On the Way

A Practical Theology of Christian Formation

Les L. Steele

BAKER BOOK HOUSE
Grand Rapids, Michigan 49516

Copyright 1990 by
Baker Book House Company
Printed in the United States of America

Library of Congress Cataloging-in-Publication Data

Steele, Les L.
   On the way: a practical theology of Christian formation / Les L. Steele.
   p.   cm.
   Includes bibliographical references and index.
   ISBN 0-8010-8309-5
   1. Spiritual formation. 2. Christian education—Philosophy. 3. Developmental
psychology—Religious aspects—Christianity. 4. Life cycle, Human—Religious
aspects—Christianity. I. Title. BV4511.S73 1991
      248.2—dc20   90-39049
                                                                CIP

On the Way

Contents

Acknowledgments

Acknowledgments are awkward to write. You feel presumptuous in assuming that people will want to be identified with what you have written. It is also impossible to identify all those persons who have in some way contributed to the development of your ideas. So with these thoughts in mind, I want to thank Baker Book House for their confidence in the project. Allan Fisher, Jim Weaver, and Linda Triemstra were quite helpful. Thank you to Seattle Pacific University, which provided time to do some of the work. To students in courses and people in churches who listened and questioned; to Ann Deibert, Patty Fox, Jeff Geers, and Bret Plate, who read the manuscript and offered valuable insights; to Bob Drovdahl, Rod McKean, and Jim Plueddemann, who read and talked about the ideas, thank you. Special thanks to Dave Nienhuis, who assisted in research, editing, and a variety of other tasks. To Gail, Chad, and Andrea, my wife and children, thank you for tolerating fits of moodiness and absent-mindedness and always helping me keep in focus what is really important.

Introduction

This book is about becoming Christian. It is about maturing in the life of Christian faith. It addresses this issue from the perspective of practical theology, theology that "enables the living community to reflect upon and guide its own action in the context of God's continuing action."[1] James Poling and Donald Miller describe practical theology as having to do with the intersections of two axes. One axis describes the importance and the balance of the social sciences and theology as they inform the practice of ministry. The other describes the relationship of church and society. As suggested by the first axis, practical theologies can be categorized according to the importance placed on either social science or theology. A critical scientific model places most emphasis on the insights of social science. A critical correlation model treats both equally. A critical confessional model appropriates the ideas of the social sciences through the lens of faith. This is to say not that a critical confessional model does not take seriously the insights from the social sciences, but that it interprets them in accord with Christian faith. The approach to Christian formation here is a critical confessional model of practical theology. It selects and understands psychological insights that are in line with Christian faith. It is also concerned with reflecting on Christian life in a way that empowers Christian formation.

My theological position is self-consciously Wesleyan. This means that I have a particular way of viewing Scripture and theology. Scripture exists to assist the church to grow in faith. Theology is practical divinity,[2] that is, it is to clarify the call of the gospel so as to empower

1. James Poling and Donald Miller, *Foundations for a Practical Theology of Ministry* (Nashville: Abingdon, 1985), p. 12.
2. Thomas Langford, *Practical Divinity: Theology in the Wesleyan Tradition* (Nashville: Abingdon, 1983).

the formation of Christian lives. This understanding of both Scripture and theology is dynamic and life-shaping rather than static and propositional. As a Wesleyan theology it is also interested in moving on in Christian faith. Often Wesleyan theology is characterized as too optimistic about the possibility of complete Christian maturity in this life. Streams of Wesleyanism have been overly concerned with the end of the journey, but much of Wesleyan theology seeks to understand the journey itself. This book stands in the stream that emphasizes the process of Christian formation.

In regard to the psychological assumptions of the book, I offer first a note of caution, then an explanation. Much of the church's activity today has become overly psychologized. The church has forgotten that it has its own story of how humans feel and act, and this story must be considered. Robert Coles decries the use of "psychological pieties" in the place of good hard prayer.[3] Richard John Neuhaus claims that Christians must "reconsider the exchange of their heritage for a mess of psychobabble."[4] I agree. Too often we hear about the need for self-esteem without a word about sanctification. We must be careful not to lose our identity as Christians, an identity shaped primarily by Scripture and Christian tradition, not by psychology.

However, we must not repudiate important insights that come from psychology. We must seek to understand optimal human development, which is the joining of holiness and wholeness. We must seek an understanding of Christian human development in which heart and mind join in love for God and neighbor. Often psychology's insights about how religion ignores reality are true. Its insights about how persons develop are essential to an understanding of how to facilitate Christian formation.

The goal of this book is to bring together the Christian story with the insights of psychology, critiqued by Christian theology, in order to describe a practical theology of Christian formation. The book describes the direction and process of being on the way to Christian formation. The word *formation* is consciously chosen. *Formation* implies that a person is in the process of being formed and at the same time is forming. As Christians our formation is a result of both God's initiative and our responsibility. We are formed as we respond

---

3. Robert Coles, "Psychology as Faith," *Theology Today* 42 (April 1985): 69.
4. Richard John Neuhaus, "Religion and Psychology," *National Review* 19 (February 1989): 46.

appropriately to God's actions on our behalf. Later I will use the phrase *Christian maturing*. As awkward as it seems, it is important to carry the idea of continuing action and not to assume that maturity is something attained. We often operate with rigid, static, mechanistic images of being Christian that cause us to live under the illusion that there is an end product. If only we will read such-and-such and do thus-and-so, then we will arrive. Then we will be disciples and be able to disciple others. My approach denies any such view. All who name the name of Christ are disciples and affect the maturing of others. We must see ourselves as always on the way.

Not only does this approach reject the mechanistic notion of Christian formation, but also it rejects any romantic notion that claims that just to live is to be about the process of becoming more Christian. Some have advocated a model of Christian life that simply calls us to have good feelings about ourselves and to feel our way to faith. That approach risks excessive subjectivism that insists that good feelings determine Christian formation. It tends to do away with the reality of human sinfulness, leaving people in the mire of directionless human experience.

The approach I advocate seeks to give direction to those who see themselves as on the way. I see people as pilgrims becoming more Christian. The story of the exodus illustrates how we are about this process. Just as the people of Israel were led out toward freedom, Christian formation leads us out toward freedom in Christ. This leading out is not directionless but aims at the promised land of the kingdom of God. It aims at Christian maturing.

Part 1 develops a theology of Christian formation out of theological reflection and consideration of biblical materials. The chapter about theology describes the criteria by which psychological notions are to be critiqued and sets forth the vision of Christian formation from a Christian theological viewpoint. The chapters on biblical material explore implications for Christian formation from the Gospels and the Epistles. Part 2 turns to psychological theory, first considering the options in psychology and, by applying the criteria set forth in the theological discussion, discerns which approaches are most useful in Christian formation. This leads to a chapter summarizing developmental theories of psychology, which in turn leads to a review of work that has made use of developmental theory in understanding Christian formation.

Part 3 then describes a practical theological approach to Christian formation. It describes faith, Christian maturity, and general principles embedded in this approach. Finally, part 4 discusses cycles of Christian formation across the life span and education for Christian formation that is congruent with the approach described.

The book serves as both an introduction to the field of Christian formation from a developmental perspective and an expansion on the field. I hope readers will be encouraged to be on the way to a maturing Christian faith.

Part 1

Theology and Christian Formation

1

The Christian Story

Primacy of Narrative Theology

We begin by exploring the themes in theology that are most important in our attempt to develop an understanding of Christian formation. I will develop the themes by way of a narrative structure. There are two primary reasons for doing this.

Understanding Persons Theologically

First, narrative theology is the most useful way of doing theology, particularly as it relates to ministry and the life of the church. Propositional theology tends to distance itself from the real lives of individuals for whom it is supposedly being done. It loses contact with real life, which should be the starting point for theology. "Without such living contact, theological doctrine readily becomes (in a pejorative sense) objective—remote from actual Christian life, a set of empty propositions more suited to attacking rival theologians than to informing the church of God."[1] This tragic lack of contact has separated theologians from laymen, harming both parties. A narrative approach may bridge the gap. We must do theology so that it touches people.

Because of its importance in our study, readers should understand what narrative theology is and how it functions. Narrative theology

1. James W. McClendon, Jr., *Biography as Theology: How Life Stories Can Remake Today's Theology* (Nashville: Abingdon, 1974), p. 178.

generally begins with a view that life is more processive or dynamic than static and is best understood as an unfolding story. This implies that our best understanding of the dynamic relationship between God and people comes through story. Canonical story, faith community story, and life story are three types of narrative useful for theology.

The first form of narrative is the canonical or biblical story. In doing narrative theology from the biblical text a literary, wholistic approach is used to interpret Scripture. It is literary in that the portions of Scripture that are narrative in form should be interpreted accordingly and, more broadly, the entire canon of Scripture should be seen not as a theological dictionary but as the unfolding story of God's relationship with the world. It is wholistic in that it takes Scripture as a whole, not fragmenting and dissecting it until its unity and internal coherence are lost.

The second form of narrative is the story of the faith community. As Gabriel Fackre states, "The narrator in this case is neither a specific textmaker nor a personal storyteller but a faith community."[2] Particular faith communities have their unique stories of how they came to be and how they see the Christian faith. The memory of these communities serves as a source for narrative theology. The task of narrative theology in this case is to look critically at the stories of particular communities in order to use them to enliven people's faith.

The third form of narrative is life story. This is the story of one's own life and faith. The man in John 9 who was healed of blindness and then grilled time and again by the Pharisees, who were attempting to make the story of Jesus fit their preconceived theological propositions, told his story when he insisted, "One thing I do know, that though I was blind, now I see" (John 9:25).

In telling and hearing personal stories of faith, our faith grows deeper. The task of narrative theology is not only telling but also critiquing these stories. Narrative theology also uses the stories of past exemplars of faith who have left us enough about themselves and their faith to allow us to enter their stories.

These stories of God's dealing with people are the sources of theology. They are particularly important for a practical theology of Christian formation that seeks to speak to real, lived experience. This leads to my second reason for using narrative theology.

2. Gabriel Fackre, "Narrative Theology: An Overview," *Interpretation* 37 (October 1983): 360.

Understanding Persons Psychologically

Narrative is not only the most appropriate way to understand persons theologically but also the most appropriate way to understand them psychologically. By using life story, developmental psychology informs us of the general patterns of human development. Erik Erikson pioneered the psycho-historical approach in his studies of Martin Luther and Mohandas Gandhi. Because narrative is compatible with our concerns for both theology and psychology it provides a way of linking the two.

Content of the Christian Story

Now, an orientation to the plot of the remainder of this chapter. In *The Christian Story*, Fackre tells the story of our faith. The book is an excellent example of narrative theology. Following Fackre's lead, James Fowler, in *Becoming Adult, Becoming Christian*, outlines seven broad chapters of the Christian story: God, creation, fall, liberation and covenant, incarnation, church, and the commonwealth of God or the kingdom of God.[3] We will consider a condensed form of Fowler's version, dividing the Christian story into two acts: In the Beginning, and In the Beginning—Take Two. This will describe, in broad fashion, what the Christian story has to say about the formation of a Christian identity. Part one has four scenes: God, creation, the fall, and covenant; part two has two scenes: incarnation and Christian identity.

Act One: In the Beginning

As Christians, we often give lip service to our Judeo-Christian heritage without fully appreciating our Jewish origins. But our story begins with the children of Israel and their unique relationship with Yahweh. Here the story of God's loving relationship with creation must begin.

Scene One: God

Genesis 1:1 states, "In the beginning when God," and as Fowler says, "we cannot get behind this starting point."[4] We can work

3. James W. Fowler, *Becoming Adult, Becoming Christian* (New York: Harper & Row, 1984), pp. 82–84.
4. Ibid., p. 82.

toward developing all types of arguments for the existence of God, and we ought to, but unless someone has some will to believe we can get nowhere in convincing him. The trouble always begins with young children who ask the nasty question, "Where did God come from?" We are so intent on their realizing that they are God's creations that we forget that they will ask the next question: "If God made us, then who made God?" We reply, "Well, no one. God just is—uh, was—well, you know!" We are usually frustrated with our attempts to answer the question, but the truth is that we cannot get behind the fact that God simply is. The Old Testament never hints at any forms of atheism. The existence of God is taken for granted. The questions for the Old Testament are, "Which God?" and "How many gods?" The story of God in the Old Testament is the story of a God who desires a relationship with creation and progressively reveals Yahweh as the one true God.

Scene Two: Creation

We affirm not only "in the beginning when God," but also, "in the beginning when God created the heavens and the earth" (Gen. 1:1). In particular we affirm that God created human life. Humanity gains its uniqueness and life from the breath of God. God "breathed into his nostrils the breath of life; and the man became a living being" (Gen. 2:7). We are God's unique and special creations, and as such we must hold a high view of personhood. This does not imply self-aggrandizement, as some who are overly concerned with self-esteem might think. Instead, it evokes reverence for the nature of our being. The doctrine of creation is significant. As Christians we often place such a high emphasis on the doctrine of redemption that we fail to recognize our condition prior to the fall, the condition toward which redemption moves us. God said that creation was good. Therefore God's redemptive actions move toward making all of creation good again. John Wesley was quite concerned with the doctrine of creation and understood conversion to be only a part of the larger picture of God's desire to restore all of creation.[5]

Not only do we understand humanity as specially created and endowed with personhood, but also we understand humanity as created in the image of God. This notion adds a sense of specialness to humanity, but it also adds several other considerations important to our discussion.

5. See Theodore Runyon, "Conversion—Yesterday, Today, and Tomorrow," a paper presented at Minister's Week at Emory University, January 17, 1984.

First, God created humanity in his image as male and female. The Christian view of male and female is equality. Only after the fall do we find any sense of submission of the female to the male. This is clearly a result of sin and is to be done away with in the new creation. The relationship between male and female must be understood as complementary. Carol Gilligan, in *In a Different Voice,* describes the relationship of maleness and femaleness as complementarity. In this relationship two equals bring differing strengths and weaknesses to humanity. Only as the two are fully embraced is full humanity understood.

Second, we must consider how we are created. Are we created perfect with no need or capacity for growth, or are we created with the drive and desire to grow and develop? Theologically, we in the Western church have followed Augustine on most issues related to the nature of persons, and we have done so here. Augustine argued that the person was born perfect but lost perfection in the fall. Irenaeus, however, argued that humanity was born with the need and capacity to grow toward God. Here is the idea that part of our being in the image of God is our innate desire to grow and change. Irenaeus was onto something here. Part of the image of God is the inherent drive toward growth that humans begin with, find marred in the fall, and forsake in their unwillingness to grow.

Third, humanity's bearing the image of God means that we are to be co-creators and co-governors. If it is God's nature to create and we are in God's image, then it follows that we are also creators. Obviously we are not creators in the same way as God, but we are creators in several other ways. One way is our ability and desire to procreate. In childbearing and child rearing, we participate in the act of creation. We also create a variety of objects, from useful tools to abstract art. These, too, display our co-creative natures. Ideas also are creations. There is beauty and grandeur in a good idea that furthers the cause of God or expands our knowledge.

We also participate in God's governing work. By this I do not intend to communicate some sort of legalistic, oppressive notion of control. What I mean is that God is active in governing the world and is drawing it toward God, no matter how slowly we may think God is doing it. We are called to participate in that governance by working toward justice and righteousness. Do not confuse this with political activity for a particular nation. It may include that, but it is much larger. Our governing requires a global perspective that transcends national boundaries to call all of the world to God's vision of justice and liberation.

Finally, we are created to be in relationship. This includes marital relationships and our being in community with others. We affirm that God is the Great Three in One—God the Father, God the Son, and God the Holy Spirit. We understand that God works in a variety of ways, but through the agency of three persons. God also affirms in Genesis that it is not good for man to be alone. This affirms the necessity to be in relationship. We realize our full potential when we are in caring, reciprocal relationships. By way of these relationships, we grow and develop. Relationships alone do not bring growth, but our interaction and commitment to those relationships do. As persons we are created to be social. That is why the church must remain a significant factor in understanding the call of God on humanity. As Augustine stated, "For how could the city of God . . . either take a beginning or be developed, or attain its proper destiny, if the life of the saints were not a social life?"[6]

Scene Three: The Fall

So far we have considered four aspects of the image of God: the complementarity of male and female, our desire to grow, our nature as co-creators and co-governors, and our need for relationships. Each of these is significant in a discussion of Christian formation. Unfortunately, they are not the last words.

Frederick Buechner writes, "We are created to serve God by loving him and each other in freedom and joy, but we invariably choose bondage and woe instead as prices not too high to pay for independence."[7] There are several issues in this statement.

The words *in freedom* and *we choose* raise the question of free will or determinism. A limited sense of human free will helps to make sense out of the biblical and theological information we have on this issue. We are created for freedom, but we are created. This implies that our freedom is limited to particular purposes. We are indeed free to choose things contrary to God's desires and our best interests; therefore, freedom is real. But our choices are limited by the nature of reality and our individual circumstances; therefore, determinism is also real. We must avoid simplistic absolutes when thinking about the issue. We are both free and determined in certain ways.

The issue is sin, which Buechner says is something we choose

6. From William Bouwsma, "Christian Adulthood," in *Adulthood*, ed. Erik H. Erikson (New York: Norton, 1978), p. 96. Originally in Augustine *City of God* 19.5.
7. Frederick Buechner, *Wishful Thinking: A Theological ABC* (New York: Harper & Row, 1973), p. 55.

despite its undesirable consequences. The story of Adam and Eve relates to us the reality of sin. Sin is several things at root. It is, as Buechner says, our attempt to assert independence; we think we are independent from God and others, and we try to behave as such. Sin, the ridiculous notion that we deserve to be independent, is at root selfishness. It is looking out for number one, paying no attention to God or others. Sin is also alienation and separation. In essence, we get what we ask for; we become separate and independent, and in doing so we suffer the bondage and woe of isolation, alienation, and loneliness. Sin devours our desire for a relationship of complementarity between men and women and leads to a male-dominated church and society. Sin also devours our desire for growth. It makes us content to stagnate; consequently, we reject the newness and change that are integral to Christian maturity. Sin persuades us that we alone are responsible for our creations, that we alone own them, be they children, artifacts, or ideas. We hold on to them selfishly and scream, "Mine, mine!" Finally, sin leads us to think that governing means dominating others, not empowering them.

Sin is indeed pervasive and sickening. It corrupts the whole essence of our nature. Humanity as God made it was good, but it has gone awry. What can we do? Nothing. Even if we tried to redeem humanity, we would fail. Our only hope is in God's continual pursuing of creation. It is in a loving God who seeks to bring us back into relationship. God had thoughts of starting over again—that's what the story of Noah tells us. But he chose to work with a remnant of the original creation because, after all, it was good.

Scene Four: Covenant

Despite humanity's sinful rebellion, God graciously works to restore relationship with creation. God calls us into covenant. Beginning with the expulsion of Adam and Eve from the Garden of Eden, we see a multitude of initiatives by God to draw humankind back to God. These calls to covenant displayed God's love, grace, and mercy. Yet humankind continually rejected them.

A covenant is an agreement between two parties. In this case, it is between God and God's creatures. Leviticus 26:12 summarizes the issue: "I will . . . be your God, and you shall be my people." As this scene develops in the Old Testament, we find the children of Israel rejecting the covenant time and again. God was grieved by their unwillingness to participate in it. God desired to restore all of creation to its original design. Just as creation was good, God was working toward a re-creation that would be good, but that was never accomplished under the old covenant.

So closes scene four of act one. In the beginning—God is, God creates, humanity sins, God covenants, humanity rejects. Where do we turn for help? If we want to describe the ideal for Christian formation, we need to deal with the ideal of God's creation of humanity. Somehow, God must go a step further to bring about a new beginning.

Act Two: In the Beginning—Take Two

Incarnation of Christ

"In the beginning was the Word," begins the Gospel of John. It is John's account of the new covenant. It is interesting that John begins his Gospel in the same way that Genesis begins. In verses 2 and 3 we find references to creation and the activity of the Word in it. In verses 12 and 13 we find references to being born of God and being empowered to become children of God because of the work of Christ. In Genesis we have the account of the first "in the beginning." In John we have the account of the second "in the beginning."

To resolve the dilemma encountered in act one, scene four, God brought about the incarnation of the Word as Jesus Christ. Nothing less would do. We must have the perfect exemplar of how to obey God. The children of Israel were called to obey and found that too difficult. Yet, "when Jesus addresses to his future disciples the peremptory invitation to follow him, this Old Testament context is recalled. Jesus is to be followed as Yahweh was followed."[8] To find our way to a restored image of God, we must commit ourselves to the person of Jesus the Christ. To do this we must "look to Jesus the pioneer and perfecter of our faith" (Heb. 12:2). The word translated *author* can be translated *leader* or *trailblazer*. He is the forerunner of faith to show us the way out of our separation from God, back into relationship with him.

Paul further helps us to understand Jesus' role as the initiator of "In the Beginning—Take Two." In Romans 5:12–21, Paul develops the idea of Jesus as the second Adam. His argument is straightfor-

---

8. Ugo Vanni, "Commitment and Discipleship in the New Testament," in *Biblical Themes in Religious Education*, ed. Joseph Marino (Birmingham, Ala.: Religious Education Press, 1970), p. 158.

ward: if by one man, Adam, sin entered the world and marred the image of God in humanity, then by the one man, Jesus, righteousness is made available once again. "Jesus' act of trusting faith, flowing from a self-sacrificing love without calculation of reward, radically heals the results of Adam's faithless act of self-seeking. The contrasts between faith and mistrust, between selflessness and self-seeking, stand at the center of the human tragedy."[9] By Jesus' work we can begin once again to think of restoration to the image of God. "'Real religion,' writes Wesley when he wants to sum it all up in one sentence, is 'restoration' by Christ to humanity of all that humanity was deprived of by the Fall, 'not only to the favour but also to the Image of God.'"[10]

We must begin any discussion of Christian formation with this background in mind. What Christian formation intends to do is to lead one to a vision of what restored humanity should strive toward. When we realize that the full image of God is our vision, then we can turn to the description of humanity as originally created in order to describe our goal.

Christian Identity

By the work of Jesus the Christ, humanity is called to a new identity. How does that new identity come about? What does it look like? Two theological doctrines, justification and sanctification, answer these questions.

Justification means being "made 'right with God' after having been 'in the wrong.'"[11] Before we can even consider developing a Christian identity we must be in Christ. This is accomplished by the work of Christ. We do not justify ourselves, but by faith we appropriate the grace of God. Justification is the forgiveness of sins that allows us to begin the development of the new self in Christ. Thomas Langford writes that justification "issues into a new birth which begins maturation into the fullness of Christian living."[12] He adds, "Those who are redeemed have been given a new nature, for they have had restored in them the image of God."[13]

9. David Smith, "Faith," in *Biblical Themes in Religious Education*, ed. Marino, p. 150.

10. Runyon, "Conversion—Yesterday, Today, and Tomorrow," p. 3.

11. Gabriel Fackre, *The Christian Story* (Grand Rapids: Eerdmans, 1978), p. 198.

12. Thomas Langford, *Practical Divinity: Theology in the Wesleyan Tradition* (Nashville: Abingdon, 1983), p. 29.

13. Ibid., p. 36.

Justification frees us to develop in this new identity, and that development is what we call sanctification. "Sanctification is built upon justification and constitutes the goal, or true end, of human life. Justification opens the way to a new life; sanctification is the heart of religion and the goal of Christian living."[14] Sanctification is the process of growing in the love of God and neighbor.

When we speak of Christian formation, we are speaking of the process of becoming what we were first intended to be and are now allowed to be by the justifying work of Christ. The work of sanctification is at the heart of Christian formation. Nothing less than the transformation of the person is the result of justification. There is no formation without transformation. Our task now is to describe the qualities of a new Christian identity. What can we say about the new life into which we have been born? For an answer, we turn to the New Testament.

14. Ibid., p. 41.

2

Christian Formation in the Gospels

The New Testament reveals the qualities of Christian identity. In this and the next two chapters, we will explore the various parts of the New Testament, beginning with the Gospels, moving to the Pauline Epistles, and ending with the general Epistles. Afterward, we will summarize the theological qualities of Christian formation that will establish the foundation for our attempt to integrate psychology and theology in order to describe an approach to Christian formation.

Why do we focus on the different canonical units to describe Christian formation in the New Testament? There is a well-known story about several blind men attempting to describe an elephant. One, who grasped the tail, said, "An elephant is like a snake!" Another, touching the ear, said, "No, an elephant is like a large tree leaf!" Another, feeling the leg, said, "Oh, no, an elephant is like a tree trunk!"

In the New Testament, similarly, we find a variety of literary types, from historical narrative, to teaching material, to poetry. We also find a variety of perspectives on the gospel event. When we focus on these, we are grabbing different parts of the whole.

This is true when we look at the understandings of Christian formation in the various canonical units. There is a diversity of perspectives, all of which combine to yield a rich, full description of Christian formation. If one perspective is taken in isolation from the others, we may begin to emphasize a unidimensional view of Christian formation to the exclusion of the whole picture. To avoid that, we will use the canonical units of the New Testament to bring into focus a whole picture of Christian formation.[1] I will also discuss a few specific issues that arise from these canonical units.

The Gospel of Matthew

The Gospel of Matthew emphasizes obedience and righteousness. Christian formation is a matter of obeying the teachings of Christ and attempting to live a righteous life. Jesus himself exemplified his call to live a righteous life. When John the Baptist balked at baptizing Jesus, Jesus said, "Let it be so now; for it is proper for us in this way to fulfill all righteousness" (Matt. 3:15). Another time he said, "Blessed are those who hunger and thirst for righteousness, for they will be filled" (Matt. 5:6).

Righteousness implies living in right relationship with God. Chapters 5 and 6 of Matthew go on to describe many practical issues of daily life and how they are to be handled in a righteous manner. How do you treat enemies? How do you treat those who ask for things? How do you understand marriage? Later in the Sermon on the Mount, Jesus says, "But strive first for the kingdom of God and his righteousness, and all these things will be given to you as well" (Matt. 6:33). Righteousness is the central theme of Matthew's Gospel. As followers of Jesus we should emulate his example of righteousness and heed his teachings on what a righteous life is.

The Gospel of Mark

Suffering stands out as a central theme in the Gospel of Mark. Mark tells us that Jesus plainly "began to teach them that the Son of Man must undergo great suffering, and be rejected by the elders, the chief priests and the scribes, and be killed, and after three days rise again" (Mark 8:31). This was too much for Peter, who rebuked Jesus. He saw things, Jesus said, from a human, fallen perspective, not from God's perspective (v. 33). To correct him, Jesus turned to the crowd and the other disciples and taught this about Christian formation: "If any want to become my followers, let them deny themselves and take up their cross and follow me" (v. 34).

1. I appreciate my colleague in New Testament, Dr. Robert Wall, for assisting me in the development of this approach.

Suffering is a prime motif for understanding Christian formation. As Dietrich Bonhoeffer wrote, "The bid of Christ is the bid to come and die." To be involved in Christian formation will cost you, perhaps even your life. We are called to be involved in Christ's sufferings. This is a theme radically different from many contemporary notions of American Christianity that emphasize the good life of American middle-class living as synonymous with Christian life.

The Gospel of Luke

Luke's Christian is the socially active disciple. People concerned about being followers of Christ are obedient to God's intentions in human history. Those intentions are for true disciples to do justice, love mercy, and walk humbly with God (Mic. 6:8). This appears first in John the Baptist's teaching. Responding to crowds asking, "What then should we do?" he replied, "Whoever has two coats must share with anyone who has none; and whoever has food must do likewise" (Luke 3:10–11). To be about the business of God means to care for the uncared-for and to show mercy. When a lawyer wanted to know how to inherit eternal life, Jesus told the story of the good Samaritan. Then he asked, "Which of these three, do you think, was a neighbor to the man who fell into the hands of the robbers?" The lawyer answered, "The one who showed him mercy." Jesus responded, "Go and do likewise" (Luke 10:25–37). Christian formation takes place in merciful acts to others.

Also involved in Luke is a social sense of mercy. It is not simply private acts of mercy that are required but public acts as well. It is no surprise that many of those who are currently working with liberation theology appeal to Luke's Gospel for support.

The Gospel of John

The Gospel of John is a call to sectarian living. The developing Christian is in the world but not of it. In Jesus' farewell discourse, this theme arises several times (John 14–17). Disciples of Christ are hated by the world, but they love one another (John 15:18–19; 13:35). Jesus prays that the Father will make the disciples one as he and the Father are one, "so that the world may believe that you have sent me" (John 17:21). There is an implicit call here to create a community apart from the world in order to be Christian together. That is sectarian living—being separated from the world.

Another distinctive of John's Gospel is the emphasis on the Holy Spirit. In no other Gospel do we get as clear a teaching on the role of the Holy Spirit for Christian formation. John gives us a spirituality of Christian formation. Here we find a mystical element in Christian formation as we see the role of the Holy Spirit as the one who will teach, guide, and comfort the followers of Jesus.

A Composite Picture

A composite understanding of Christian formation in the Gospels yields a picture of Christian identity as a life of righteous living according to Jesus' teachings. A difficult life, it is marked by self-denial and care for others through acts of mercy and justice. Christian life is not privatized but lived for the sake of all humanity.

Christian life also calls us together in community with others who love and support one another in our efforts to live as Jesus lives. Within the community of faith the Holy Spirit operates, empowering Christian formation.

As a whole, the Gospels present a powerful and compelling call to a life quite different from what the world admires. The composite picture is well-balanced, including inward and outward spirituality. It shows us a life that is both private and public.

There are also several specific characteristics of Christian formation throughout the Gospels that I would like to address. These describe developing Christians by way of the attitudes and behaviors they exhibit. They describe not only outward attitudes and behaviors but also ways of seeing things or making sense out of our experience.

The Great Commandments

When asked what was the greatest commandment, Jesus responded, "'You shall love the Lord your God with all your heart, and with all your soul, and with all your mind, and with all your strength.' The second is this, 'You shall love your neighbor as yourself'" (Mark 12:30–31). Herein lies the essence of true religion. John Wesley states, "Does the love of God constrain thee to serve

Him . . . ? Is thy heart right toward thy neighbor? If thou art thus minded, may every Christian say, yea, if thou art but sincerely desirous of it, and following on till thou attain, then thy heart is right. . . ."[2] Contemporary Christianity often loses sight of these commandments and finds itself caught up in vast amounts of legalisms, formulas, and complicated rationalizations. Jesus' words must stand in the front of our efforts to describe Christian formation. They are at the core of the gospel. It is in relation to these that all the following concerns of Christian formation must be considered.

The Kingdom of God

A central teaching of Jesus is the kingdom of God. The parables typically begin with the phrase, *The kingdom of God is like.* Jesus also said that the kingdom is in our midst. This implies what George Eldon Ladd called the "is but not yet" nature of the kingdom. We sometimes emphasize the "not yet" with our preoccupation with eschatology and the coming kingdom. This is indeed a reality, but it is one that is beyond our control. The "isness" must also inform our idea of Christian formation. By creating a vision of the coming kingdom and realizing that we are to work toward it, we find ourselves drawn by the story of the kingdom. Martin Luther King, Jr., said, "I have a dream," and that dream compelled him in his efforts for civil rights. We too should say, "I have a dream"—a dream of the kingdom of God that shapes the way we live.

Self-Denial

Over and over again in his statements on what it takes to be his disciple, Jesus speaks of the need to deny self. "If any want to become my followers, let them deny themselves. . . . For those who want to save their life will lose it, and those who lose their life for my sake, and for the sake of the gospel, will save it" (Mark 8:34–35). An important characteristic of Christian formation is the willingness and disposition to deny oneself.

Walter Conn asks, "What, then, is an authentic Christian under-

2. John Wesley, "Catholic Spirit," in *The Works of Wesley*, ed. Edward H. Sugden (Grand Rapids: Francis Asbury, 1955), vol. 2, pp. 138–39.

standing of self-sacrifice, if it is not the sacrifice of self? Quite simply, Christian self-sacrifice consists in the denial of all those (otherwise perhaps quite legitimate) desires, wishes, and interests of the self which interfere with the singleminded commitment to follow Jesus in love."[3] Christians are called to give up their desire to be self-grounded persons. Being self-grounded implies attempting to look out for number one and satisfy our own wishes. Today the church too readily assimilates pop psychology's emphasis on self-groundedness. Somehow we have latched onto the idea that you must love yourself before you can love others; thus, we have become more concerned with self-esteem than with sanctification. There is a psychological need for self-love, but we have bought the secular formula instead of the theological formula to satisfy it. The secular formula places self on center stage, while the theological formula insists that in giving we receive, that in loving others we find ourselves, that in losing our lives we save them. Christian formation does not aim at self-actualization but at self-transcendence, which comes through our painful attempts to deny ourselves and care for others before and above ourselves.

We must be careful, however, not to misunderstand self-denial. According to William Stringfellow, "the whole notion of self-denial or suppression of self, associated with a purported spirituality, is really a matter of self-indulgence, a vainglorious idea, a superficial 'spiritual' exercise at most."[4] Stringfellow may overstate his case, but his point is well taken. All we need to do to see why is to imagine monastic or contemporary forms of self-denial that may become roads to self-aggrandizement. Many times we flaunt our spirituality by acts of supposed self-denial when all we are really doing is currying the praise of men (Matt. 6:1–2). Self-denial is a habit of the heart. Jesus warns us that a spirituality worn on our sleeves is nothing more than horn blowing. Our self-denial, therefore, is an attitude of the heart that seeks the kingdom of God first in all of our daily activities.

A companion of self-denial is suffering. Handling suffering is an essential part of Christian formation. Our concern here is not with the reason for suffering but with how we handle it. Although we do not always understand why suffering takes place, God does, and he does not take it lightly. Ultimately he can explain it all. Meanwhile,

3. Walter Conn, *Christian Conversion: A Developmental Interpretation of Autonomy and Surrender* (Mahwah, N.J.: Paulist, 1986), p. 21.

4. William Stringfellow, *The Politics of Spirituality* (Philadelphia: Westminster, 1984), pp. 40–41.

our proper attitude toward suffering should reflect the observation by Walter Brueggemann: "Evangelical faith is also candid and unflinching about hurt, loss, grief, and endings in human history which are real and painful and not covered over."[5] A part of self-denial is the ability to deal honestly and openly with suffering, to look it square in the face, and go on our way in faith.

Service

A theme that also appears throughout the Gospels is service. In Mark 10:45 we find the words of Jesus concerning the role of service in the mission of the Son of Man: "For the Son of Man came not to be served, but to serve." In the Sermon on the Mount, he said, "Give to everyone who begs from you, and do not refuse anyone who wants to borrow from you" (Matt. 5:42). Service, generosity, and hospitality characterize Christian formation. We serve others not to create networks or so that someone owes us something, but simply because someone is in need. The good Samaritan exemplified this type of hospitality. He cared for someone at his own risk and expense with no expectation of repayment.

Childlikeness

Jesus also says that the kingdom of God is for those who come to it like a child (Mark 10:15). But let us not misunderstand. Childlikeness is "not the supposed virtue of childish 'innocence,' which is more accurately named ignorance, inexperience, and naiveté."[6] We often use the excuse of childlikeness to keep ourselves subservient to a repressive style of Christian faith. We refrain from asking questions or thinking on our own because that is not being "childlike." What we are really doing is, as Daniel Helminiak put it, keeping ourselves ignorant. Jesus had something else in mind when he spoke of childlikeness.

William Bouwsma beautifully discusses six qualities of childlikeness.[7] First, childlikeness is spontaneous. Children can do things on the spur of the moment. They have a sense of freedom about their

5. Walter Brueggemann, *Hope Within History* (Atlanta: John Knox, 1987), p. 100.
6. Daniel A. Helminiak, *Spiritual Development: An Interdisciplinary Study* (Chicago: Loyola University Press, 1987), p. 78.
7. William Bouwsma, "Christian Adulthood," in *Adulthood,* ed. Erik H. Erikson (New York: Norton, 1978), pp. 91, 92.

behavior. Second, children always anticipate growing up. They recognize that life is going to bring them a wealth of experience. Third, children have a keen way of asking simple yet profound questions. "Who made God?" "Where do people go when they die?" Children freely ask the "impertinent" questions that adults have learned not to ask even when they want to for fear others will think they are ignorant. Fourth, children readily express wonder and astonishment. I remember doing the old salt-on-string-in-ice trick for my children. When they pulled up the string and the ice followed, their eyes and mouths dropped in wonder! Even simple things evoke a sense of wonder. Fifth, children have a confident trust in life. They are not wary, like adults, when encountering new situations. Adults have become so concerned with potential danger that they often miss out on tremendous life experiences. Finally, children love to play. They can make a game out of anything. They enjoy and laugh at the things of life. They do not take things too seriously. We adults, particularly Christians, take ourselves too seriously. Life and faith are serious, but they are to be confronted with zest and playfulness that illustrate our enjoyment of this life combined with our eager expectation of a better life to come. The Talmud states, "A man will have to give account in the judgment day of every good thing which he might have enjoyed and did not."[8] To grow as children of God means to reappreciate the qualities of childlikeness.

Simplicity

Also in the Sermon on the Mount, Jesus takes up the theme of simplicity. He exhorts us not to be anxious over food, clothing, and stature. Why? Because God knows our needs and will take care of them (Matt. 6:25–34). These verses may have inspired the old Shaker song that begins, "'Tis a gift to be simple, 'tis a gift to be free." Although in the context of the Sermon on the Mount in Matthew simplicity refers to monetary issues, we should seek simplicity in our use of time, energy, and all other resources as well. Our culture measures people's worth by how busy they are. We even have car phones so that we don't waste any time in our busyness. If our calendars are full, then we must be persons of worth. In contrast to such a culture, we must seek simplicity if we wish to develop in our Christian lives.

8. Quoted in Gabriel Moran, *Religious Education Development* (Minneapolis: Winston, 1983), p. 99.

What is simplicity? It is a willingness to disentangle ourselves from too many commitments, relieve ourselves of the debts and obligations that keep us anxious and burdened. It implies that we release the control we think we have over money, time, and career. It is not total disengagement from life, but it does imply an honest estimation of what each of us can do without losing our primary focus on God. Yet simplicity is not advocating simplism. Life and faith are complex, and every person is different; we all must decide individually what simplicity means in our lives. The theme of simplicity appears in most of the classic writing on spirituality.[9] It is an issue that we must consider if we are concerned with our formation as Christians.

Peacemaking

"Blessed are the peacemakers, for they will be called children of God" (Matt. 5:9). Peacefulness in Christian life means resisting violence and conflict on all levels: personal, communal, and global. The Gospels teach that a non-resistance approach to life is part of Christian formation. But life is complex, and we are members of two kingdoms. That makes life very difficult. It is why there is diversity of opinion in regard to military issues.

Yet we must take the call of peace seriously. Is our basic impulse to engage in conflict or to look for nonviolent ways to resolve disputes? Peace is more than simply the absence of conflict. Augustine defined it as the tranquility of order. It involves a sense of harmony, right relationships, and unity of heart and mind. Peace is the environment in which life and relationships can thrive. The Hebrew *shalom* captures well this wholistic conception of peace. Does our life exhibit peace?

The Holy Spirit

These themes and characteristics or qualities may sound like a shopping list of things to strive toward. It may sound as if attaining these characteristics makes us well-formed Christians. This is not the case. They are central characteristics and qualities that the Gospels call us to embody in our formation as Christians. But they are not

9. See Richard J. Foster, *Freedom of Simplicity* (New York: Harper & Row, 1981), and Søren Kierkegaard, Purity of Heart, trans. Douglas Steere (New York: Harper & Row, n.d.), for good examples of these works.

mechanistically applied behaviors. In the Christian life we often feel as if we must strive for our formation. We push ourselves to mature as Christians. But Neill Hamilton characterizes this as an early and immature stage of Christian life.[10] A more mature Christian life "is drawn ahead by the Spirit rather than driven from behind by the self."[11]

Here we see the cooperative nature of Christian formation. We are active agents in our spiritual growth, but the Holy Spirit is also active in the process.

How, according to the Gospels, does the Holy Spirit cooperate in Christian formation? First, the Spirit is in us to transform us. He remakes us in the image of God. Second, he assists us in fulfilling the great commandments. As John Wesley states, we "are taught by the Holy Spirit to love God and neighbor with a love which is springing up to everlasting life."[12] Third, the Holy Spirit helps us to pay attention to our Christian lives. This happens in the common routines of life.

Many times, when we think about the role of the Holy Spirit, we conjure up ideas that are beyond the ordinary and miss the Spirit's subtle leading. Francis Buckley and Donald Sharp suggest different marks of his working: "The Spirit of Truth makes us sensitive to true values, so that these can guide our lives. The Spirit calls our attention to alternative lines of action that have escaped our notice. Thus the Spirit sharpens our critical faculties and enables us to weigh more carefully the information we possess."[13] In a similar vein, Oswald Chambers writes, "The Holy Spirit further leads us into the will of God by influencing our mental processes as we submit our minds to His control. John Wesley testified that God generally guided him by presenting reasons to his mind for acting in a certain way."[14] This view of the work of the Holy Spirit is more natural in that it stresses the cooperation of the Holy Spirit in the process of becoming a new creation. It appears to be deeply rooted in a strong commitment to

10. Neill Hamilton, *Maturing in the Christian Life: A Pastor's Guide* (Philadelphia: Geneva, 1984).

11. Ibid., p. 29.

12. John Wesley and Clare G. Weakley, *The Nature of Spiritual Growth* (Minnesota: Bethany House, 1977), p. 85. Originally from John Wesley, "The First Fruits of the Spirit."

13. Francis J. Buckley and Donald B. Sharp, *Deepening Christian Life* (New York: Harper & Row, 1987), p. 29.

14. J. Oswald Sanders, *In Pursuit of Maturity* (Grand Rapids: Zondervan, 1986), p. 171.

the doctrine of creation. We do not need to look for the marvelous manifestations of the Holy Spirit, although they may happen. We can be assured that the Spirit is active in our daily lives as we seek to love God and our neighbors.

In the Gospels we find a diversity of perspectives and specific emphases about Christian formation. The Gospels recognize that the Christian life is related specifically to the person of Jesus Christ and calls us to particular ways of living and thinking.

3

Christian Formation in Paul's Writings

We turn now to the writings of Paul and a description of what they bring to our understanding of Christian formation. An encapsulation of Paul's ideas on Christian formation yields five ideas.

First, Paul is concerned about orthodoxy, or right belief. Paul institutionalizes the church, so we expect to find in his work an emphasis on getting the facts right. Scattered throughout Paul's writings are teachings on the orthodox views of Christ's nature, the resurrection, and the work of the Holy Spirit. For Paul, to be about the business of Christian formation, you must be concerned with orthodox belief.

Second, however, Paul refuses to limit Christian formation to right belief. Right belief is necessary but not sufficient. Paul is also concerned about the role of the Holy Spirit in Christian life. Not only orthodox belief about the Holy Spirit but also correct understanding and abundant experience of the Holy Spirit's work is important to Christian maturity.

Third, Paul is concerned about the role of the faith community in Christian formation. The body of Christ is important in Paul's theology because it contributes to both Christian maturing and carrying out God's will on earth.

The fourth and fifth emphases, vision and process, are central to Paul's teaching on Christian formation. Paul began his Christian journey with a conversion experience on the road to Damascus. The idea of being on the road, or in process, is an appropriate summary of Paul's teaching and life. He was always on the road as he worked to spread and establish the gospel. His ideas of the vision and process of Christian life are captured well by the phrase *on the road*. Vision grasps the goal of our Christian life. It is the end or purpose that we journey toward. Process is how we travel toward the vision. In many ways the distinction is arbitrary. It is difficult to separate vision from process. The vision is the process and vice versa, or the journey is the destination. Nevertheless, for clarity's sake, we discuss them separately.

Paul's Vision of Christian Formation

Knowledge and Love

Essential to Paul's vision of Christian formation is the goal of being fully known by God and filled with God's love. For the Ephesians Paul prays "that Christ may dwell in your hearts through faith, as you are being rooted and grounded in love. I pray that you may have the power to comprehend, with all the saints, what is the breadth and length and height and depth, and to know the love of Christ that surpassses knowledge, so that you may be filled with all the fullness of God" (Eph. 3:17–19). Paul envisions Christian formation as composed of our complete renewal according to the image of God so that we can enjoy the rich fellowship with God that we are intended to have. For us to have that, Christ must dwell in our hearts.

In many texts Paul uses the phrase *in Christ* to speak of our current standing as Christians and our desired standing as we continue to develop in our relationship with Christ. We grow more into Christ by becoming more Christ-like. We are called to grow up to the "full stature of Christ" (Eph. 4:13). As William Bouwsma states, "Conformity to this loving Christ is the goal of human development."[1] We "are being transformed into the same image" (2 Cor. 3:18). Christian formation, for Paul, is being increasingly like Christ. We are to imitate his thoughts, words, and deeds. We are to imitate his example of self-emptying (Phil. 2:5–8). Growing as a Christian often means giving up, for the sake of Christ and others, what might rightly be ours.

1. William Bouwsma, "Christian Adulthood," in *Adulthood*, ed. Erik H. Erikson (New York: Norton, 1978), p. 90.

Freedom and Liberation

Paul's vision of Christian formation also includes a keen sense of freedom and liberation: "For freedom Christ has set us free" (Gal. 5:1). Paul felt deeply the freedom that comes in Christ. Prior to his Damascus road experience, he was committed to the Jewish law as a way of showing his love and commitment to God. This could be an oppressive way of living. But when Paul came into Christ, he became a champion of the freedom and liberty that are ours in Christ. Being free himself, Paul was determined to help other believers to recognize their liberty and release in Christ.

The gospel is not an oppressive message but a liberating one. For this reason, Christians can exhibit freedom from the worry and anxiety usually associated with a legalistic and compulsive style of religion. Too often, today's literature on Christian formation gives the impression that to develop as Christians we must submit our entire beings to some discipler or some compulsive system that demands a legalistic and rigid approach to all of life. Paul opposes any system or person who would oppress the Christian, who is freed to be formed in Christ.

Growth in Christ-likeness

Paul's vision of Christian formation emphasizes growth. The Christian life is always in process. In Ephesians 4:11–16, Paul calls us to move from infancy to adulthood. "Christianity has, then, a conception of full adulthood," writes Bouwsma; "the goal of human development is total conformity to the manhood of Christ. But since this is a transcendent goal, the practical emphasis in Christian adulthood is on the process rather than its end."[2] If we are no longer to be infants, and if full adulthood is a transcendent goal, then we are somewhere in between; we are adolescents. Adolescents are characterized by their openness to growth and their questioning of the future. Adolescents ask, "What will I be when I grow up?" Adolescents are open to possibilities and willing to explore alternatives.

Christians who are open to growth are much the same. They ask what they will be or where can they grow or what they can do next. Their attitude is that the future is open and they are willing to make changes where needed.

In Philippians 3:12–15, Paul states his concern for striving for

2. Ibid., p. 85.

perfection, or completeness. One legitimate way to interpret these verses is that Paul is referring to progressive or processive perfection or maturity. In verse 12, he writes that he has not already obtained maturity nor has "already reached the goal. . . ." But in verse 15 he writes, "let those of us then who *are* mature . . ." (emphasis added). Perfection, completeness, or maturity, then, is not a static condition that we obtain once and for all. Instead, it is dynamic, open, and changing. It is a qualitative process that continues so that Paul can call on those who are perfect to press on to perfection.

Paul's vision of Christian formation includes our call to know and be filled with the love of God, to grow in Christ-likeness, to experience freedom, and to realize that Christian formation is a process.

The Process of Christian Formation

Does Paul give us any clues as to the nature of the process? How does one develop in the Christian life? Paul offers no simple formulas. There are not four or ten steps to Christian formation; he gives us no simplistic theory of discipleship. Christian formation is a difficult, thoughtful involvement with all of life during which one must seek to pay attention to God. "The Christian life, then, is conceived as indefinite growth, itself the product of a full engagement with temporal experience involving the whole personality."[3]

Development

Paul concentrates on three issues that are important to the process. First, the process is developmental. Throughout his letters, Paul uses developmental images to illustrate the nature of Christian life. We must grow from infancy to adulthood, moving from milk to meat. His illustrations point to a model that recognizes a developmental and natural approach to Christian growth.

Central to this process of development is the attempt to give oneself away. Not only is self-emptying a part of Paul's vision of Christian formation, it is also a key feature of how the developmental process can take place. As we empty ourselves, we are more able to be filled by Christ. The more we are sacrificial in lifestyle, the more we can develop from our sinful self to the new creature that Christ has

3. Ibid., p. 87.

created in us. Developmental psychological theory speaks of the process of decentering as an aspect of development. This is the same idea: moving away from self as central to placing Christ and others in the center.

The Body of Christ

Second, Paul emphasizes the role of the body of Christ, or faith community, in Christian formation. Paul's key thought on the body of Christ, in 1 Corinthians 12–14 and Romans 12, is that the members of the body are there to build each other up and, by so doing, to build up the body. We contribute to one another's development by using whatever talents or gifts we have to strengthen the body of Christ so that we all aspire to the full stature of Christ (Eph. 4). Christian formation occurs as we interact with a faith community. We cannot mature in our faith apart from fellow believers.

The Holy Spirit

Third, Paul emphasizes the role of the Holy Spirit in Christian formation. The Holy Spirit confirms in us that we are children of God (Rom. 8:9–16), assists us in prayer (Rom. 8:26–27), and comforts and convicts. The Spirit works in us to bring about growth. Paul writes, "The one who began a good work among you will bring it to completion by the day of Jesus Christ" (Phil. 1:6). The Holy Spirit cooperates with us in our attempts to form a Christian life. Paul reveals an interesting tension in this when he writes, "Work out your own salvation with fear and trembling; for it is God who is at work in you . . ." (Phil. 2:12–13). We are to work it out, but God is at work in us. We find here an emphasis on our partnership with the Holy Spirit in Christian formation. It will not take place without our cooperation, and we cannot achieve it alone.

The Holy Spirit cooperates in the process by giving us gifts to use for the development of the faith community. Notice again the interaction necessary for Christian formation. It is a triadic relationship among the individual, the Holy Spirit, and the faith community. Gifts are not given for self-edification but for the edification of the body. If gifts are given for the body, then each individual must be connected to the body in order to receive the benefits of the gift. In like manner, the body cannot receive the gifts of the Spirit without the involvement of each Christian. It is, therefore, in the interaction of these three that the Holy Spirit works for the development of the Christian and the body of Christ.

According to Paul, the Holy Spirit does, however, work for the individual by cooperating in producing spiritual fruit. In Galatians 5:22–23, Paul lists the fruit of the Spirit, each element of which is a quality of personal character. The evidence of the Holy Spirit operating in our lives is the presence of these qualities. They are essential to Christian formation.

Sometimes we attempt to use or create these fruits mechanistically. We treat them as if they were a bag of virtues to be carried about, as if they were products of a Christian finishing school. Nothing could be farther from Paul's concern. Character is our basic orientation toward life. It is "a person thinking, reasoning, believing, feeling, willing, and acting as a whole."[4] Character forms as we respond to the vision of the Christian gospel and interact with the Christian community. It is defined by our vision, which empowers action that, in turn, also forms our character.

The qualities of character that Paul lists—love, joy, peace, patience, kindness, goodness, faithfulness, gentleness, and self-control—are formed in us with the cooperation of the Holy Spirit. The Spirit works within us to transform us, to give us gifts, and to develop character.

The process of Christian formation as found in Paul's letters consists of an emphasis on the process of development, the importance of interaction with the faith community, and the cooperative role of the Holy Spirit. The process assists us in our journey toward the vision of Christian formation.

4. Craig Dykstra, *Vision and Character: A Christian Educator's Alternative to Kohlberg* (Mahwah, N.J.: Paulist, 1981), p. 59.

4

Christian Formation in the General Epistles

Now we consider some of the non-Pauline letters: Hebrews, James, and 1 and 2 Peter. Whereas Paul tends to place more emphasis on orthodoxy, or right belief about the nature and work of Jesus, the non-Pauline material tends to place primary emphasis on orthopraxis, or right action or practice. Not all action is orthopraxis. Orthopraxis is thoughtful, reflective action motivated by the grace of God and responding to a desire to love God and neighbor. It is not enough to believe correctly; one must live correctly.

The Epistle to the Hebrews

The call to be steadfast pilgrims is the focus of the teaching on Christian formation in the Epistle to the Hebrews. The image of Christian life as pilgrimage is nothing new. It is found in both Testaments. It is an important image for Augustine, Luther, and Wesley and in a great many hymns. Who can forget the line, "This world is not my home, I'm just a-passin' through"? Or the black spiritual, "Swing low, sweet chariot, comin' for to carry me home"? Pilgrimage is an image in much of our classical spiritual literature; John Bunyan's *Pilgrim's Progress* is an example.

Lewis Sherrill discusses three images or metaphors of life.[1] Life

1. Lewis J. Sherrill, *The Struggle of the Soul* (New York: Macmillan, 1954).

can be viewed as either treadmill, saga, or pilgrimage. If treadmill, we live a most dreadful existence. Viewed this way, "life is a squirrel cage or a weary grind."[2] Saga is appealing, with its romantic sound of the old West. It adds a dimension of adventure and meaning. But as Sherrill points out, it tends to be overly humanistic. It is the rugged individual living alone without need for anyone, particularly God. Pilgrimage, on the other hand, is a life journey lived before God. It is infused with meaning no matter what the circumstances.

In Hebrews, both Christians and Jesus himself are seen as pilgrims. Jesus is the pioneer, author, and finisher of our salvation (Heb. 2:10; 12:2). He could be called our pathfinder or trailblazer. He leads the way for the pilgrim people. As we engage in Christian life as pilgrimage, we know that someone has gone before us. Jesus serves as our model and guide. "For Christians, growth is not indiscriminate change," write Francis Buckley and Donald Sharp. "It is a deliberate movement into the future, following the trail already blazed for us by Jesus Christ."[3]

A Journey into the Unknown

What is the nature of the Christian pilgrimage?

Christians are strangers or aliens in a foreign land, waiting expectantly for the city of God (Heb. 11:9–10). Wandering about and persecuted (vv. 37–38), they long for a better homeland (vv. 14, 16).

The pilgrimage has some clear characteristics. First, it is a journey into the unknown. It is not, "as in the mystery religions, an immediate entrance into a safe harbor but rather, though its direction has been established, the beginning of a voyage into the unknown."[4] We have a promise that the journey will lead us to the city of God, but we have no idea how to get there or what it will be like when we arrive. Second, the Christian pilgrimage is a risky journey. We risk possessions, health, family, and self as Christian pilgrims, and the risk is threatening as it calls us into the unknown. "For we are always travelling," says Luther, "and must leave behind us what we know

2. Ibid., p. 4.

3. Francis J. Buckley and Donald B. Sharp, *Deepening Christian Life* (New York: Harper & Row, 1986), p. 134.

4. William Bouwsma, "Christian Adulthood," in *Adulthood*, ed. Erik Erikson (New York: Norton, 1978), p. 87.

and possess, and seek for that which we do not yet know and possess."[5] This is particularly difficult for those who feel as if they have arrived at a complete view of God, for they are unwilling to be called beyond this point.

A Hazardous Journey

The journey is difficult and dangerous, without promise of safety or comfort. We are not exempt from the realities of earthly living, from the pain of death and suffering, from the injustice of rape and child abuse. We are sojourners in a foreign and alien land and are subject to its sinfulness. But we take comfort in knowing that we are not alone in the journey. We travel with a host of faithful fellow sojourners from the past (Heb. 11). The "pilgrimage of faith must be made in the company of others," writes Sharon Parks.[6] In all honesty, we recognize that this can be both comforting and discomforting. We need to encourage and support one another in our journeys, but we also risk the danger of group think, the force that a group has over each of its members to create destructive attitudes and actions. The children of Israel supported one another but also encouraged one another in grumbling and idol making.

An Unfulfilled Journey

Finally, the journey leads to an unfulfilled destiny, at least when viewed from a temporal perspective. Hebrews 11:13 teaches that the past giants of faith all died without having received what was promised. Moses never dwelt in the promised land but died outside it; nonetheless, as Hebrews indicates, he anticipated the city of God. Our journey culminates in the heavenly city on the other side of this existence. This is comforting, yet it leaves us in the precarious position of living without reward in this world. It puts a strain on our ability to persevere when no rewards are in sight. However, glimpses from afar of the promised city of God encourage us. Our pilgrimage includes an unknown future, risk, harsh treatment, the blessings and curses of a communal journey, and an unfulfilled destiny this side of eternal life.

5. Cited in *Luther: An Introduction to His Thought*, ed. Gerhard Ebeling, trans. R. A. Wilson (Philadelphia: Fortress, 1970), p. 162.

6. Sharon Parks, Walter Brueggemann, and Thomas Groome, *To Act Justly, Love Tenderly, Walk Humbly* (Mahwah, N.J.: Paulist, 1986), p. 33.

The Christian pilgrimage is similar to the movements identified as parts of cultural rites of passage. Arnold Van Gennep speaks of three movements in a rite of passage.[7] First, there is a period of separation in which the child, about to become an adult, is isolated from the community. Then comes a period of transition in which various trials are encountered, most having to do with the skills required to be a fully functioning adult in one's culture. Finally, there is incorporation as the child-turned-adult is welcomed back into the community with a new identity. These three movements characterize the Christian pilgrimage as well. We are separated from the world and become aliens. For the rest of our earthly lives, we are sojourners, tested and tried in preparation for our incorporation into the city of God, which at last we enter only after we leave this world behind.

To journey through hazards into the unknown and unseen, Christian pilgrims must be steadfast. Hebrews 12 exhorts us to consider the "cloud of witnesses" who have persevered to the end. With them, we are called to "run with perseverance," to "endure trials for the sake of discipline" (vv. 1, 7). "Therefore," the writer urges, "lift your drooping hands and strengthen your weak knees" (v. 12). We must be steadfast and endure. Consistency and stick-to-itiveness are hallmarks of successful pilgrims.

The Epistle of James

The Epistle of James stands out as the most praxis-centered letter of the New Testament. While Paul emphasizes orthodoxy—right faith and doctrine—James emphasizes orthopraxy. In Paul's letters we learn that salvation is by grace through faith apart from works (Rom. 3:28; Eph. 2:8–9); in James we learn that real saving faith bears fruit in good works (James 2:14–26). Scripture is rich with diversity, and Christian faith is developed as we appreciate the various emphases of the biblical writers. James connects particularly with both the Gospel writers and the Old Testament wisdom tradition in his contributions to our understanding of Christian formation.

Four themes from James pertain to our discussion: orthopraxis, perseverance, wisdom, and simplicity. Each of these can be considered a quality of character. Remember, character is not only espoused virtues or mere behaviors but the sense of self derived from

7. Arnold Van Gennep, *Rites of Passage*, trans. Monika B. Vizedom and Gabrielle L. Caffee (Chicago: University of Chicago Press, 1960).

our vision of Christian maturity, and it is exhibited in both attitude and behavior.

Orthopraxis

For James, orthopraxis is the key to true and mature religion. In James 1:22–26, we find an outline of true Christian formation. We are to be doers of the word, not mere hearers, who delude themselves. As an example of persons who are mere hearers, James describes those who look at themselves in a mirror and, immediately after leaving it, forget what they look like. James does not refer to physical appearance but to the quality of a person. Mere hearers may have the superficial appearance of a Christian, but they have not allowed the reality of the gospel to penetrate their lives. As a result, they deceive themselves when they claim to be followers of Christ.

Works, or right behavior, must be the natural consequence of being true believers of the word. Works are the ethical response to God's grace in our lives. In 1:27 James defines pure religion as caring for those for whom no one else cares and who cannot care for themselves. He refers to orphans and widows as chief examples of such people. They are powerless and forgotten. If our religion does nothing to apply the power and ability we possess on behalf of the powerless, it is worthless. It is also worthless if it does not lead adherents to keep themselves "unstained by the world." We need to keep ourselves aware that the Christian value system differs radically from the competing value systems of the world. Although the differences are many, the context implies that one important difference is in how we deal with the powerless. We must, in very practical, daily ways, resist being molded into the patterns of this world, which are abusive of persons.

James 2:14–26 furthers the call to orthopraxis. If we say that we have faith and do not care for those in need, our faith is dead. Some argue that faith implies only proper belief. James retorts that by that definition even the demons are orthodox! They believe that God is one. No, orthodoxy by itself is meaningless for James. There must be a corresponding transformation in behavior and character.

One can readily see how James would ruffle the feathers of those who are most focused on justification by faith alone. His response would be that they have an improper definition of faith. Faith cannot simply mean orthodoxy or right belief; it must include orthopraxis or right behavior, or else it is not faith.

Perseverance

James also calls for perseverance in faith. Believers should "consider it nothing but joy" when they encounter trials (James 1:1–4). Joy focuses not on the trial but on the resultant perseverance. If we persevere, endure, and remain steadfast or faithful, we will be on our way to perfection. The word for perfection here is *teleios*, which denotes completeness or maturity. It is the goal toward which we aim and work. We are to persevere and endure trials not because we enjoy pain but because we have a vision of the kind of persons we believe God is calling us to become.

James 1:12 again sounds the theme of perseverance or endurance through trials. To persevere is to persist in spite of opposition or discouragement. It is to stick to it. Lewis Smedes, in *Caring and Commitment*, refers to commitment as "sticking to what you're stuck with."[8] In our vision of Christian formation, the perfection to which we aspire is something we're stuck with, so we must stick to it. We must realize that Christian formation is not the easy way but the right way. For this reason perseverance and endurance must mark our character.

Wisdom

James is also concerned with connecting Christian formation with the practice of wisdom. James 1:5 states, "If any of you is lacking wisdom, ask God. . . ." There is an obvious connection here with the Old Testament wisdom tradition, particularly Proverbs. Proverbs 2:3–6 connects wisdom with understanding, discernment, integrity, justice, and knowledge. Wisdom is a quality of life, thought, and action that empowers Christian living. What are some of the characteristics of wisdom in James? Wisdom brings stability to persons. It allows us to withstand the forces that would push us away from our Christian lives. It brings accurate self-knowledge. We are able to objectively assess our life situations. In particular, James connects with the wisdom tradition when he refers to control of the tongue as a quality of wisdom. He calls us to be quick to listen and slow to speak (1:19–20). If we cannot control our speech, we lack wisdom. Self-control is also important. Wisdom enables us to control not only the tongue but all aspects of our lives.

8. Lewis Smedes, *Caring and Commitment: How We Learn to Love and Live* (New York: Harper & Row, 1988), p. 14.

Simplicity

Finally, James is concerned that Christian formation include simplicity. In 2:1–5, James condemns materialism and champions poor believers. James reflects the wisdom and prophetic traditions exemplified in Micah 6:8: we are called to do justice, to love kindness, and to walk humbly with God. James also connects with the gospel's theme of simplicity in regard to material wealth. Jesus is hard on the rich, warning them that attachment to riches can prohibit their entering the kingdom (Matt. 19:23–24). To be concerned about Christian formation we must resist the materialistic impulses of the world.

But simplicity refers to more than money. James Fenhagen states, "Simplicity reflects an inner wisdom and a comfortableness with the wholeness of life that is bred in solitude and expressed through certain spontaneity and joyousness that enriches every gathering in which it is found."[9] Simplicity is a quality of character that reflects a peacefulness and comfortableness with our lives.

The Epistles of Peter

The epistles of Peter contribute two primary thoughts to our discussion of Christian formation: holiness and suffering. First Peter 1:13–16 states, "Therefore prepare your minds for action; discipline yourselves; set all your hope on the grace that Jesus Christ will bring you when he is revealed. Like obedient children, do not be conformed to the desires that you formerly had in ignorance. Instead, as he who called you is holy, be holy yourselves in all your conduct; for it is written, 'You shall be holy, for I am holy.'" The call is to blamelessness and sinlessness. We are to be sanctified or set apart for God's use.

Holiness

The language of holiness has been so confused with moralism and particular theological frameworks that it is either repulsive or dismissed because of theological myopia. The biblical call to holiness has faced three primary problems.

9. James C. Fenhagen, *Ministry and Solitude: The Ministry of Laity and Clergy in Church and Society* (New York: Seabury, 1981), p. 68.

First, holiness has, in some circles, become nothing more than mere moralistic behaviorism. It is a set of do's and don'ts that a particular subculture finds it convenient to affirm. William Stringfellow is concerned to correct the idea that sanctification is "some sentimental or pietistic or self-serving notion of moral perfection."[10]

Second, many people have begun to see holiness as something that is achieved once and for all. This is most true in the Holiness traditions that emphasize what they refer to as a second work of grace. These groups treat the experience as an act complete supposedly in and of itself; they consider the person holy from the point of this event. These groups trace this idea to John Wesley, who indeed placed considerable emphasis on the necessity of sanctification. Yet Stanley Hauerwas, a theologian in the Wesleyan Methodist tradition, has argued that the word *perfection* has come to convey too much of a sense of accomplishment rather than continued growth, "which is at the heart of Wesley's theological account of sanctification."[11] According to Hauerwas, Wesleyan groups that reduce Wesley's account of sanctification to a static event do so in spite of Wesley's own emphasis on dynamic, continuing growth in holiness.

Third, holiness is detached from the entirety of our lives. This takes two forms. The first is that our Christian lives are roped off from the rest of our lives. We do not connect our spirituality with our emotional and physical well-being or associate our Christian formation with our work and family worlds. Such compartmentalization of holiness renders it useless. Holiness implies a total renewal of the whole person. As Stringfellow writes, "In becoming sanctified and being sanctified, every facet, feature, attribute, and detail of a person is exposed and rejuvenated, rendered new as if in its original condition again, and restored."[12] Or, as Hauerwas puts it, "perfection can be characterized only by reference to the wholeness of a human life."[13]

The second form of this detachment is the removal of holiness from the social arena. We make holiness something private and individual with no connection to how we live in the broader social context. "Christian holiness in our age," wrote Thomas Merton, "means

10. William Stringfellow, *The Politics of Spirituality* (Philadelphia: Westminster, 1984), p. 33.

11. Stanley Hauerwas, "Characterizing Perfection: Second Thoughts on Character and Sanctification" (unpublished paper in author's possession), p. 2.

12. Stringfellow, *The Politics of Spirituality*, p. 41.

13. Hauerwas, "Characterizing Perfection," p. 7.

more than ever the awareness of our common responsibility to cooperate with the mysterious designs of God for the human race."[14]

With these three problems in mind we must ask, "What does holiness call us to be and become?" It is essential for Christian formation
that we have a "depiction of the life of holiness that is compelling
and attractive."[15] That depiction should not present holiness as mere
moralism, as static, or as separated from the totality of our lives.
Instead, Fenhagen points to six characteristics of an attractive definition of holiness.[16]

First, holiness is connectedness. By connectedness, Fenhagen
means single-minded attention to the call of the gospel. Hauerwas
writes that "Christian perfection is singleness of intention and constancy of character."[17] Second, holiness is able to create what Fenhagen calls 'neutral space'. By this he refers to situations in which
people can hold opinions and ideas without fear. Can we allow others to express themselves without fear of our judging them? Can we
help create settings where the subtle message is "this is a safe place"?
Third, holiness requires kingdom vision. Is the vision of the kingdom of God always informing my attitudes and actions? Fourth,
holiness bears fruit in compassion. It can suffer with others who suffer. Fifth, holiness implies righteousness, a care for justice and "right-
wiseness." Holiness seeks to make right what is not right, to make
just what is unjust. Sixth, holiness grows in companionship. It is not
something we work out in isolation for ourselves. We work it out in
community with and for others as companions along the way.

Suffering

A second theme in Peter's epistles is suffering. The saints endure
and suffer various trials (1 Pet. 1:6; 5:9–10; 2 Pet. 2:7–9). Peter consistently teaches that suffering is not good in and of itself but can be
a source of Christian formation. Most commentators agree that these
letters were written when there was actual, physical persecution.
Their lessons on suffering, therefore, were of immediate value to
their original recipients. For many Christians today who do not experience martyrdom, the message is still important. We have no right

14. Thomas Merton, *Life and Holiness* (New York: Doubleday, 1963), p. 10.
15. Hauerwas, "Characterizing Perfection," p. 12.
16. James C. Fenhagen, *Ministry and Solitude: The Ministry of Laity and Clergy
in Church and Society* (New York: Seabury, 1981), p. 68.
17. Ibid., p. 10.

to expect to escape from suffering, but we are to work toward transforming suffering for the sake of Christian formation.

For those first addressed by the Petrine Epistles, suffering was due to their affirmation of Christian faith. This kind of suffering seems to be more understandable than physical suffering brought on by illness or a sinful world. But Peter's lessons can apply to all forms of suffering.

Suffering does occur and is no respecter of persons. Too often Christians naively attempt to argue away the realities of personal and social suffering, but, as Walter Brueggemann states, "the true evangelicals are those whose eyes notice the hurt and whose noses smell the grief."[18] The task of Christians is not to deny the reality of suffering but to acknowledge it and realize that, although we may not completely understand why it exists, we must seek to overcome it and grow through it. For Peter, suffering has the potential to shape our faith. Again Brueggemann writes, "The crucial hinge in this faith formation is the pivotal power of pain."[19] What will we do with suffering that most often is meaningless and revolting? Will we simply resign ourselves to it, whether personal or social, or will we seek to transform ourselves through suffering and change the structures that bring it about?

James Loder, in *The Transforming Moment*, writes of the necessity of negating the negative.[20] When we encounter suffering we are faced with a choice: we either resign ourselves to it and so are defeated by it, or we try somehow, through the power of the Holy Spirit, to be transformed by it.

The paradigmatic example of suffering is the cross of Christ. In no way was Good Friday a good Friday. It was a horrible day with no redeeming qualities. But by negating or working through the suffering, Christ was transformed and therefore we can be transformed. Our approach to suffering should be the same. Peter teaches us to respond to suffering in such a way that we can be transformed and formed by it. We may not understand why suffering occurs, but we can face it squarely as an opportunity for the formation of our faith and character.

In our survey of Hebrews, James, and the epistles of Peter, we have learned of pilgrimage and the call to steadfastness (Hebrews);

18. Walter Brueggemann, *Hope Within History* (Atlanta: John Knox, 1987), p. 97.
19. Ibid., p. 19.
20. James E. Loder, *The Transforming Moment: Understanding Convictional Experiences* (New York: Harper & Row, 1981), pp. 161–89.

of the centrality of orthopraxis, perseverance, wisdom, and simplicity (James); and of holiness and suffering (Peter). Orthopraxis, or right action, and character formation stand out in the non-Pauline letters. They are concerned with an honest approach to the realities of life through which we can be formed as Christians.

In chapters 2–4, I have argued that four themes stand out for Christian formation. First, Christian formation is a process. It is not something to be achieved once and for all or to be ignored because we are justified by faith. Throughout the history of the church our theology and interpretation of the Bible have called us to grow in faith, to realize that there is something to which we are called and toward which we have a responsibility to strive. Second, we do not strive for growth in isolation. At one level our striving is a cooperative effort between ourselves and the Holy Spirit. We are formed by the Spirit's activity and by paying attention to it and contributing to it. At another level, the community of faith is the setting for the formation of our faith. We do not develop in isolation from other people. If we neglect relationships, our faith will suffer. Third, Christian formation is involved in and aware of the realities of life. It must not be compartmentalized into a separate section of our lives; we are not to neglect the social dimension of faith. Faith is formed and transformed as we encounter the realities of life with openness and honesty. Fourth, Christian formation is concerned with belief, behavior, and attitude. As Theodore Runyon has spoken of it, Christian formation combines orthodoxy, orthopraxy, and orthopathy.[21] It is not enough to believe the right things, or to do the right things, or to feel the right things. Our wholistic Christian faith demands all three.

The task before us now is to develop an approach to Christian formation that integrates the theological and biblical aspects of Christian formation with a developmental psychological perspective.

21. Theodore Runyon, "Conversion—Yesterday, Today, and Tomorrow," a paper presented at Minister's Week, Emory University, January 17, 1984, p. 11.

Part 2

Psychology and Christian Formation

5

Three Forces of Psychology

In this chapter we will discuss the contribution of psychology to an understanding of Christian formation. To do so, we must first consider the various approaches to psychology, then decide which approach will be most helpful in understanding Christian formation. We will discuss psychoanalytic, behavioristic, and humanistic/self approaches to psychology. In each case, we will consider the basic theory and the manner in which the religious dimension is approached and then critique the theory in the light of four questions: preservation of the person, compatibility with a Christian world view, ability to explain, and usefulness in understanding Christian formation and (in particular) education for Christian formation. *Preservation of the person* refers to the necessity of a high view of personhood that is a part of the Christian view of persons.[1] *Christian world view* refers to a theory's ability to include a notion of transcendence and the positive and necessary contribution of religion. *Ability to explain* speaks to a psychological theory's ability and power to explain everyday general life issues. This may include the ability to predict behavior, but it need not. Finally, we are interested in the *usefulness* of a theory for shaping education. How can the theory inform educational ministry?

Frank Goble wrote *The Third Force* to introduce readers to humanistic psychology.[2] This assumed that there were two psycho-

1. C. Stephen Evans, *Preserving the Person: A Look at the Human Sciences* (Grand Rapids: Baker, 1977).
2. Frank G. Goble, *The Third Force: The Psychology of Abraham Maslow* (New York: Grossman, 1970).

logical forces preceding humanistic theories. Those forces were psychoanalytic psychology and behavioristic psychology. (There are varieties and hybrids of the theories that are not reflected in the following discussion.)

Psychoanalytic Psychology

A psychoanalytic approach to psychology begins with Sigmund Freud.[3] All theories arise in particular cultural settings and historical moments, and this is true of Freud's psychology. His work began in the strict Vienna culture. The strictness focused on sexuality and the need to be quiet about its pleasures. Freud began by exploring the physiological roots of hysterical behavior. His work led him to believe that many problems people faced resulted from difficult childhoods and sexual repression. It also led him to focus on the importance of the unconscious in the development of persons.

Three Key Components

Freudian psychoanalytic theory can be summed up in three key components: the dynamic, the structural, and the sequential. The dynamic component refers to Freud's notion that persons have instinctual drives that must be satisfied or sublimated. These are the result of psychic energy that is not dissipated but transferred or transformed into something else in the person. (Freud seems to have derived this idea partly from work in physics at his time that emphasized the conservation of energy.) The primary purpose of the energy is to care for our instinctual needs and drives. Those instincts demand satisfaction and gratification. As individuals grow, they must deal with the conflicts that occur due to culture and themselves in regard to these drives. They begin to realize that there are appropriate and inappropriate times to satisfy the drives, and they must deal with this realization. But the energy does not disappear, since energy is conserved, so it must be refocused or redirected. This leads to the structural component in Freudian theory.

The structural component is the part of Freudian thought that is

3. See Sigmund Freud, *New Introductory Lectures on Psychoanalysis,* ed. and trans. James Strachey (New York: Norton, 1933).

most widely recognized. Most people know the terms *id, ego* and *superego*. These, according to Freud, are the structural parts of personality. We are born with only id, which may be called the pleasure principle or the "go" side of our personality. Id seeks gratification and does not consider or even know that gratification may come at the expense of someone else. Infants crying to have their hunger needs met in the middle of the night have no idea that this is in conflict with their parents' need for sleep. It is for the most part an unconscious aspect of our personality. It is here that psychic energy works toward gratification in the first years of life.

But at some point infants begin to realize that their desires do conflict with other persons' and that tensions arise over these conflicts. This gives rise to the second structural component, which is the superego. The superego may be imagined as the "no" component in contrast to the id as the "go" component. As children become increasingly aware of the reality of other persons with their desires and of parental norms and rules, they realize that the id must be regulated if they are to survive. The superego arises from the conflict of the id with these competing desires.

To arbitrate this usually unconscious or subconscious conflict, the third component of the personality develops: the ego. The ego is what you see, that is, the conscious, public knowledge that people have of themselves and that others know them to be. Ego is what you see when uncontrolled desires are disciplined.

Finally, there is the sequential component. Here Freud gives us a first glimpse at a type of developmental sequence through which individuals pass. Freud describes the first phase as the oral phase, for he believes that infants first attempt to deal with their psychic energy, and perhaps their desire to know, with their mouths. This is followed by the anal stage, in which children fixate on their ability to control elimination of waste. Then there is the phallic stage, in which Freud assumes that interest turns to the genitals. After this there is a period of latency in which the libido or sexual energy takes a rest to be displaced later by the genital stage.

These, briefly, are the major actors in Freud's script of the human personality. His theory centers on the unconscious. It focuses on internal conflict, in that ego is worked out in the battle between id and superego. It is laden with sexual overtones and cultural artifacts from a somewhat culturally circumscribed era.

Psychoanalysis and Religion

Freud was an atheist, which clearly shapes his critique of religion. Three elements of Freud's approach to religion shape his ideas of the origins and psychology of religion.[4] First, he was committed to an evolutionary understanding of life and religion. In his day, cultural anthropology began to understand religion in evolutionary terms. It held that religion had gone through at least three phases: pre-animism, animism, and totemism. Pre-animism is belief in mysterious forces and powers but not in particular spirits. Animism is the beginning of religion, with belief that everything has a soul. This belief in the ensoulment of all life led to a belief in spirits that still dominates many primitive cultures. Totemism is the belief that a particular animal or plant protects the tribe and may include the sacrifice of the totem.

Freud finds in this progression a movement from magic to religion. Now, he believes, with further evolution, we are in a scientific phase that exposes the falsity of all religion. His work in this area is most clearly stated in *Totem and Taboo*.[5]

Second, Freud's view of religion was rooted in his explanation of the Oedipal crisis. As Hans Küng states, "Thus religion is based entirely on the Oedipus complex of mankind as a whole."[6] Individuals must conjure up a father figure to replace their real father and to deal with guilt arising from the desire to possess their mother sexually.

Finally, Freud believed that religion was nothing more than illusion or wishful thinking. People wish for knowledge of the origins of life, confidence in a moral order, protection, and life after death. Out of these childish wishes religion develops its illusory power.

Clearly, Freud was not friendly to religion. But we must not too quickly discount the insights he offers us in correcting immature religion. We do sometimes re-create a father figure out of God; that is, we re-create God in our image to satisfy our own needs. We also engage in wishful thinking. Much of the prosperity theology of the 1980s and of the past is rooted in a wish-fulfilling drive.

4. See Sigmund Freud, *Totem and Taboo,* trans. James Strachey (New York: Norton, 1950), The Future of an Illusion (New York: Doubleday, 1961), and Moses and Monotheism, ed. Katherine Jones (New York: Vintage, 1939). See also Hans Küng, Freud and the Problem of God, trans. Edward Quinn (New Haven: Yale University Press, 1979).
5. Freud, *Totem and Taboo.*
6. Küng, *Freud and the Problem of God.*

Critique of Psychoanalytic Theory

We are now ready to critique psychoanalytic theory, applying as our standard the four criteria set forth at the start of this chapter.

First, the responsible agent is lost to psychoanalytic theory. Persons seem to be the product of both their genetic endowment and the psychic environment in which they are nurtured. Although there appears to be some sense of person, there is no clear sense of a conscious, active person. Second, psychoanalytic theory is far removed from a Christian world view. Freud's commitment to atheism prohibits his understanding the world as a creation of God. Psychoanalytic psychology is also unable to describe psychological processes. Without falling into simplistic reductionism of complicated psychic processes, we can readily see that Freud's preoccupation with the unconscious and his complicated approach to all situations renders his theory less than useful in interpreting everyday life. This means that his theory is also less than adequate for understanding education. Very little in Freudian psychology is useful in designing a theory of education. There may be some help in its insight into particular student behaviors, but it offers virtually nothing in considering teaching, curriculum, and other components of education. Overall, there is little to commend psychoanalytic theory's contribution to understanding Christian formation. We can, however, use its view of religion in understanding how immature religion may operate.

Behaviorism

Behaviorism is rooted in the work of John B. Watson, Ivan Pavlov, and B. F. Skinner.[7] Of these we hear most about Skinner. They all hold in common a commitment to a purely scientific view that led to the doctrine that human life is no different from animal life. Persons are all alike and are best understood as machines. That is, humans are simply made up of a series of lawful operations that can be reduced to their various elements. This leads to the primary notion of behaviorism, which is that people are products of their environments. Human development is shaped solely by the environment. At this point, a distinction must be made between Pavlov and Skinner.

7. For a concise summary of behaviorism, see Neil Salkind, *Theories of Human Development* (New York: Van Nostrand, 1981).

Pavlov's view is categorized as classical behaviorism. Classical behaviorism looks for the connection between a response and the stimulus that caused it. If you were given five dollars apparently out of the blue, you would begin trying to discern why. You would look for the stimulus that was responsible for the behavior so that you could replicate it. This is difficult due to the complexity of stimulus/response relationships. One way to avoid this is to ignore the stimulus and concentrate on observing the behaviors that you wish to see continued and rewarding them. This, in essence, was the process Skinner proposed. His theory is called operant conditioning and concerns itself with the response-reinforcement sequence. All you need to do to shape desirable behavior is to reward it when it occurs. For Skinner, therefore, development is a change in the possibility that a behavior will occur again. This development is the result of the environment as it offers reinforcers to condition behavior.

Denial of Feelings

Another major tenet of Skinner's behaviorism is the denial of inner states or feelings. In his autobiography Skinner writes, "I also do not think feelings are important."[8] Skinner holds Freud responsible for our preoccupation with inner states or feelings. He believes that these are nothing more than our attempts to give a name to how we deal with our environment.

Skinner's view of religion is similar to Freud's. For Skinner, God is a construct not of our Oedipal complex but of our culture. We create God mostly to control behavior. We use the God idea to suppress behavior that we do not want, to reward behavior that we do want, and to manipulate people into being the kind of people we can control. Skinner does not invest as much energy into denying God as does Freud; nevertheless, he denies that God exists. Again, we may think that Skinner offers us no help in understanding Christian formation, yet much of our work in Christian formation is grounded in unrecognized behaviorism. Old-fashioned appeals to Christian growth work on guilt to manipulate behavior and claim that real Christian growth is found primarily in behavioral change. Discipleship programs do much to shape behavior to conform to the behavior of those in leadership. We begin to talk, act, and look like a "discipler."

8. B. F. Skinner, *A Matter of Consequences: Part Three of an Autobiography* (New York: Alfred A. Knopf, 1983), p. 399.

Critique of Behaviorism

Behaviorism discounts the idea of personhood. Persons are responsible in that they must respond to the environment, yet this is not true responsibility but mere reaction. More than any other psychological approach, behaviorism eliminates the idea of the responsible self. Persons no longer can be held responsible for their actions because they are simply responding to environmental stimulae.

Behaviorism also rejects the Christian world view. God is a cultural construct; therefore, a theistic world view is simply the construction of prior cultures.

The most compelling aspect of behaviorism is its ability to interpret and explain behavior. No doubt we all enjoy our "warm fuzzies." We do react well to positive reinforcement, and our behavior does tend to be modified by a regular schedule of such reinforcements. Behaviorism is useful in explaining what happens, but it can say nothing of what ought to happen. It cannot deduce what is right and good. This void is filled by a supposedly value-free approach to shaping culture. This entire approach becomes suspect when we realize that someone must decide what culture will be like. If the presuppositions of behaviorism are accepted, then it is very useful. If, however, you reject its primary assumptions, then its usefulness is limited.

Behaviorism is used extensively in educational technology. It is most effective with the mentally handicapped. Learning machines are also a result of behaviorism. These allow someone to sit at a computer and simply answer questions given by the program. If the student answers correctly, the machine moves on to the next question. The obvious assumption is that the concept of the question has been learned, since the student answered correctly. The problem with this approach is that learning becomes the mere ability to give a correct response without explaining how the answer was found or what difference the information might make.

Behaviorism is the tacit psychology behind most of our current Sunday school curricula. Behavioral objectives are found in them, and children are thought to have learned if they display the expected behavior. I recall walking into one children's Sunday school class where the teacher was going from student to student and having them say, "Jesus loves me." When I looked at the day's lesson in the curriculum, I found that the behavioral objective was that each student would be able to say, by the end of the lesson, that Jesus loved her. The teacher was ensuring that the lesson was "successful" by having the children recite the words. Whether they understood or believed what they said hardly mattered. The majority of our discipleship approaches are also built on a tacit behaviorism. We are to act in particular ways that supposedly exemplify our discipleship.

In summary, behaviorism is useful in understanding Christian formation primarily by its recognition that we do respond to positive reinforcement. Its ability to guide us, however, is very limited due to its loss of personhood and incompatibility with the Christian world view.

Humanistic/Self Psychology

The third force in psychology is humanistic or self psychology. The term *self psychology* carries the basic notion behind these theories, that is, the centrality of the self or person. Those who represent this approach—Abraham Maslow, Carl Rogers, Gordon Allport, Victor Frankl, Erich Fromm, and others—hold that there is in all persons a self that is the core of being.[9] This self seeks to be actualized. Persons have two basic drives: the drive to survive and the drive to actualize. The survival drive includes the need for food, shelter, and safety, or maintenance needs. Self-actualization is a drive toward things that enhance life.

Self Psychology's View of the Person

Maslow asserts that self-actualized persons exhibit six characteristics.[10] First, they must have survival needs met before they can even begin the work of actualizing. Second, they have a realistic perception of the world. Third, they accept themselves, others, and the natural world. Fourth, they are spontaneous. Fifth, they are intimate. Finally, they have a sense of humor, creativity, and nonconformity. These tendencies come and go but are characteristic of persons who are engaged in self-actualizing. So-called peak experiences are also related to self-actualization. They remind us that the characteristics just described are not static. All people have within them the

9. See Salkind, *Theories of Human Development*. See also Salvatore R. Maddi, ed., Personality Theories: A Comparative Analysis (Homewood, Ill.: Dorsey, 1968).

10. See Abraham H. Maslow, *Toward a Psychology of Being*, 2d ed. (New York: Van Nostrand, 1968).

groundwork to be self-actualizing. This indicates that self psychologies are maturationistic.

Self Psychology and Religion

Psychologies of the self are much more open to a religious dimension of life than either psychoanalysis or behaviorism. Not all who affirm self psychology affirm the reality of God and religion, but most do not aggressively oppose it. Several self psychologists are strong advocates of a sane approach to religion. Allport has contributed much to an understanding of religious maturity. In *The Individual and His Religion*, Allport discusses six characteristics of religious maturity.[11] A mature religious perspective is well differentiated—the believer can distinguish his beliefs from others'. It is dynamic, driving the person. It is consistently directive. That is, the dynamism is not directionless but moves toward a particular goal. It is comprehensive, which implies that someone observing the individual can see how the religious dimension is woven into all of his life. It is also integral, or central to each part of life. The image of a tapestry is helpful when considering these last two characteristics. From the top (comprehensive), you can see the beautiful picture with the threads forming a coherent design. From beneath (integral), you discover the individual threads that make up the picture. Some persons' religious commitments appear to be woven into all of life, yet when you investigate you find that the tapestry unravels. Finally, a mature religious sentiment is heuristic. It is tentative and open to change. There is something sad about people who think they have all the answers wrapped up and cannot consider alternative viewpoints.

These characteristics are useful in designing an approach to Christian formation. They also show that some self psychologists are not only open to religion but have done much to help us understand the relationship between self and faith.

Critique of Self Psychology

It is clear that the notion of personhood is preserved in these theories. The person is their foundation. At least to this extent, these

11. Gordon Allport, *The Individual and His Religion* (New York: Macmillan, 1957).

theories are compatible with Christian faith. However, the theories also tend to place too much emphasis on the person. Some place so much weight on the idea of personhood that any need for a transcendent God is greatly diminished.

Self psychologies also tend to be compatible with a Christian world view. They do not all affirm God and religion, but they tend not to be antagonistic toward them either. They are also somewhat useful in describing how we should act toward persons. If we all have at our core this self, then we should treat one another with respect. Self psychologies, therefore, give us insight into daily human relationships and counseling technique.

Finally, education has received much direction from these theories, particularly from the work of Rogers.[12] Self psychology sees education as much more than merely accumulating facts or modifying behavior. Education is the attempt to facilitate a person's drive toward self-actualization. A teacher is one who guides and directs the student toward learning but does not make the student learn. Teachers know their own feelings and limitations and are willing to be vulnerable about them with students. These ideas are much more attractive than a behavioristic approach, but possibly too much so. That is, the theory is, in general, too optimistic about persons, and that carries through to its educational implications.

12. Carl R. Rogers, *Freedom to Learn: A View of What Education Might Become* (Columbus, Ohio: Bobbs-Merrill, 1969).

6

Developmental Psychological Theories

Each of the three psychological theories has something to offer to our consideration of the human personality from a Christian perspective. The theories within the humanistic/self school are probably the most attractive because of their focus on the person. Yet they, like all the others, are inadequate. We need an overarching theory that will give a clearer picture of the person. Such an approach needs to take into account the reality of sin and suffering. These issues are largely absent from self psychologies because of their overly positive estimate of human nature. Within behaviorism, sin and suffering do not matter much, since the person has no control or responsibility. Within a psychoanalytic approach there is suffering but no sin.

Also, none of these theories adequately describes growth across the entire life span. Psychoanalytic theory comes the closest, yet it is limited to childhood and early adolescence. Behaviorism cannot understand the qualitative distinctions of various ages. It treats age differences as merely quantitative, that is, a matter of adding the behaviors necessary to be adult. In some ways it is reminiscent of the ancient homunculist theory, which held that the fetus was simply a miniature adult in need only of physical, quantitative growth. It saw no difference in thought or emotional processes between a child and an adult. Similarly, humanistic theories have no clear idea of development across the life span. They seem to be open to a continual process of growth but have not considered distinctions through time. In some ways, self psychology is a theory of the adult because the idea of self is a fairly complicated notion that assumes that its subjects are reflective persons.

We must also locate the genesis of development in each of the theories. Is it nature or nurture? The nature/nurture question asks, "Who is responsible for growth and development?" Psychoanalytic theory sees development as an interactive process but eventually places primary responsibility on the environment. Behaviorism is so committed to nurture—the environment—that all responsibility is left in the hands of culture. Humanistic theories are overly optimistic about the individual's abilities to grow and actualize; they downplay the complexity of persons and their cultures.

Each theory has something that commends it, yet the deficiencies suggest that we look for another theoretical option. We need a psychological theory that is aware of the dark side of human nature—of both sin and suffering; one that will allow a description of the quantitative and qualitative changes that occur across the entire life span; one that views human development as an interaction between nature and nurture, since that seems to be much more the case when we observe real life.

That option is the field of developmental psychology. While there are similarities between developmental psychology and the other approaches, in that they share similar components, developmental theory is not narrow but is broad enough to capture many of the subtleties of real life. This chapter will consider developmental psychology and briefly summarize the major theories in the approach.

Analysis of Developmental Theories

The primary emphasis of the developmental approach is the person in process across the entire life span. Early developmental theory concentrated on the developing child. As the approach matured, it began to take into account development during adolescence and, finally, adulthood.

It is interesting to trace this development, particularly in the work of any one theorist. Erik Erikson, for instance, began in 1950 with *Childhood and Society,* adding *Youth: Identity and Crisis* in 1968 and then *Adulthood* in 1978.[1]

1. See Erik H. Erikson, *Childhood and Society* (New York: Norton, 1950).

Erikson and other theorists describe general stages and phases of development across the life span. These stages are predicated on the assumption that there is a typical pattern of human development that we all tend to follow. Granted, individual differences greatly influence this pattern, but we can still describe general patterns. Developmental theories also assume that development occurs as an interaction between individuals and their environments. It is not the same as a humanistic approach, which tends to overemphasize the maturational issues, or behaviorism, which overemphasizes cultural issues. It is dynamic and interactive. Individuals act on culture as much as culture acts on them. The direction of this development is from less complex to more complex. How we think, feel, and act becomes much more complex as we develop. Individuals are also seen as developing from more egocentric to less egocentric perspectives. Children are egocentric in that they have a difficult time realizing that others have perspectives and desires different from their own. Healthy development makes us more sensitive to others' views, desires, and needs.

Two major theoretical perspectives constitute developmental psychology: structuralism and functionalism.[2] Structural-stage theories focus primarily on the structure of thinking or how thinking is done, not on what is being thought about. Jean Piaget's work in cognitive stages is the foundational theory of structuralism. His work, as we will discuss later, focuses on how individuals construct knowledge or make sense out of experience. The concern is not so much *what* people think as *how* they think. Functional theories, however, focus on the content of emotional life or the life decisions being made. While structural theories concentrate on *how* we think, functional theories focus on *what* we think or experience. Erikson is the foundational theorist of functionalism.

An example may help. From the perspective of functionalism, adolescents are at what Erikson refers to as the identity versus identity confusion stage. They must make decisions about their identity and their sense of self. From the perspective of structuralism, adolescents are at what Piaget calls the formal operations stage, when they can think about thinking. These two theories describe two aspects of adolescents that make up the whole. That is, adolescents will not be able to define their identities adequately without the ability to

2. See Lawrence Kohlberg, *The Psychology of Moral Development*, vol. 2 of *Essays on Moral Development* (New York: Harper & Row, 1984), pp. 491–97.

think reflectively. Therefore, using both theories renders the best understanding of various stages.

We must be careful, however, not to collapse the theories into one approach. Erikson's stages are quite different from Piaget's. All of Erikson's stages are traversed by everyone. They are related to chronological development. Piaget's stages, however, are not so chronologically related. There are ages when certain stages are most likely, but one does not automatically traverse each of the Piagetian stages; people may fixate or stop at any particular stage. These two theoretical approaches do not speak of the same thing. They address two different aspects of human development and must be taken together, not collapsed into one. Neither should one be selected over the other.

Structural Theories

Given this brief distinction between the structural and functional theories, let us attempt now to understand major theories in each approach. In examining structural theories, we will give an extensive summary of Piaget, then briefly describe several other structural theories.

Jean Piaget

Jean Piaget began his academic professional life in biology. His early work centered on how organisms adapt to their environments. He studied the albino sparrow, attempting to see if there were some adaptive function to albinoism. He was also interested in a broad range of subjects and enjoyed philosophy. He soon began working with intelligence tests, and through that work he became fascinated with the ways persons attempt to understand the world. He was not interested in what a person knew but in how she thought about what she knew. This led him into a lifelong study of what he called genetic epistemology, the study of the development of how persons come to know.

Two ideas are basic to Piaget's theory of cognitive development. First, Piaget asserted that humans have a natural tendency to organize the various stimuli that they encounter. He called this the organizational tendency. As words, ideas, and experiences come into our lives, we try to organize them in some type of mental structures. Second, persons have what Piaget called the adaptation tendency. This refers to their tendency to adapt to their environment. We desire to make sense out of our environments. This is what we see in the natural curiosity of infants, who must explore everything—often to their parents' dismay. Piaget claimed that persons attempt to organize and adapt in two ways: assimilation, by which we attempt to fit new information into existing categories, or accommodation, by which we create new categories when no category exists for the information in question.

Based on these assumptions, Piaget describes four stages of cognitive development. These stages are not closely connected with chronological age, although there are typical age periods associated with them. Piaget's theory is interactionist, positing that cognitive development results from people's active engagement with the environment. Cognitive development is not maturationally determined; if the environment does not provide the stimulus needed for further development, the development will not occur. The stages follow an invariant sequence and are hierarchical. No one can move from pre-operational thinking to formal operations without passing through concrete thinking. Thus, the order of these stages and of the stages of other structural-developmental theories is the same for everyone. The stages are also hierarchical, which implies that a higher stage is better than a lower stage. This creates problems with structural theories, but it remains a basic component of them. It does not imply that lower stages disappear altogether but that they are incorporated into the higher stages.

The first stage Piaget describes is sensorimotor cognition. This form of cognition is found in infants from birth to about two-and-a-half years of age. Infants try to make sense out of their world through their senses. They use sight, sound, smell, touch, and taste to understand the variety of stimuli in their surroundings. Their manipulation of objects displays their own cognition and causes their parents' despair. The second stage is pre-operational thinking, which is typical of children two to seven years old. By calling this stage pre-operational, Piaget implies that thinking has not taken on logical operating patterns. It is intuitive and magical. There is no need to make sense in a conversation with a child at this stage, because in many ways what you will have is not a conversation or dialogue but simultaneous monologues in which you discuss different things while appearing to have true dialogue. At this stage children also tend to attribute life to inanimate objects like favorite dolls or stuffed animals. This may be related to the beginning of nightmares at this age as things begin to move in the dark.

Following this stage comes concrete operations, usually around ages seven through eleven. Now logical operations can take place: two plus two must equal four, and new experiences are assessed in relation to prior experiences. These operations, however, are limited to concrete experiences. Dennis the Menace exemplifies concrete thinking at its best. In order to make sense out of ideas, these children must tie them to real experience and not some hypothetical possibility.

After this comes the final stage Piaget described, called formal operations. This typically occurs beginning around age eleven or twelve. Piaget has described this stage as "thinking taking wings," or thinking about thinking. It is the ability to apply logical operations to hypothetical situations or, in the best sense of the phrase, possibility thinking. This stage is the last discussed by Piaget. Some have speculated about further stages of development within formal operations, such as the move from problem-solving to problem-posing thinking or from dialogical to dialectical thinking.[3]

Following is a brief description of other structural-developmental theories. This is not an exhaustive account of these theories but a glimpse at how the approach can be used in a variety of areas of human development.

Lawrence Kohlberg

Kohlberg used the structural-developmental notions of Piaget to build a theory of moral development. Beginning with his doctoral work in 1958 and continuing to today, he has elaborated a theory of the stages of moral development. More accurately, it is a theory about the development of moral reasoning as an aspect of morality. Kohlberg is interested in how persons think about moral decisions. He is interested not in *what* persons decide but in *how* they decide. How they make moral decisions reveals their particular moral stage.

Building on John Dewey's three levels of morality, Kohlberg identifies two stages in each.[4] The stage persons are in is identified by conducting a semi-clinical interview in which the interviewer presents moral dilemmas to them and listens to the reasoning behind their responses. Following is a brief description of each stage.

3. See the discussion of dialectical thinking in James W. Fowler, *Becoming Adult, Becoming Christian* (New York: Harper & Row, 1984). See also Patricia Arlin, "Cognitive Development in Adulthood: A fifth stage?" *Developmental Psychology* II (1975): 602–6.

4. See John Dewey, *Moral Principles in Education* (Carbondale, Ill.: Southern Illinois University Press, 1975).

Level 1—preconventional. At this level, moral reasoning revolves around questions of good and bad or right and wrong, and these are understood in terms of physical consequences. Good behavior will bring reward and bad behavior will bring punishment. The power of those who apparently make the rules is also considered.

Stage 1: This stage is oriented around obedience and punishment. The physical consequences of an action determine its rightness or wrongness.

Stage 2: This stage is pragmatic. Right actions satisfy one's own wishes.

Level 2—conventional. At this level, maintaining the desires of one's group is most important. One must be loyal to one's family or country no matter what the consequences.

Stage 3: This stage is most often described as the "good boy/nice girl" stage. Right behavior is what pleases one's significant others.

Stage 4: This is the stage of social conformity. Right behavior maintains social order and respect for authority.

Level 3—postconventional. At this level, one attempts to define right and wrong apart from self-interest and social groups. This is a stage of moral autonomy in which one reasons morally on the basis of universal principles.

Stage 5: This is a stage of social contract in which persons recognize the limits of social rules but abide by them, assuming that they were constructed with special respect for individual rights. It is in many ways a legal point of view.

Stage 6: This is principled morality. The person at this stage reasons on the basis of a self-chosen system of ethical principles. Central to these is justice.

Kohlberg's theory has generated much debate. Many people think that it is too narrowly focused on reasoning, others that the research is problematic, and so on. One thing is clear, however: you cannot read about moral development without reading about Kohlberg. His theory has proven useful as a lens on moral development, which is a central concern for Christian formation.

James Rest and Robert Selman

Several people have pushed Kohlberg's work in different directions. James Rest has attempted to develop an objective test of moral reasoning.[5] In it, a person responds to objective statements about

5. James R. Rest, *Development in Judging Moral Issues* (Minneapolis: University of Minnesota Press, 1979).

moral situations, and the responses determine a score of principled moral reasoning. The test is widely used as a measure of moral reasoning in the Kohlbergian sense.

Robert Selman has attempted to develop a theory of perspective taking based on the structural-developmental theory of Kohlberg.[6] By *perspective taking* Selman means the ability to understand a situation from the perspective of another. In essence, Selman asserts that perspective taking develops from a more egocentric perspective to a more mutual perspective. This is essentially the development of a person's ability to "walk a mile in someone else's shoes."

Carol Gilligan

Of special significance is the work of Carol Gilligan.[7] Gilligan challenges the male bias of the majority of psychological work, in particular Kohlberg's. She finds it significant that both Kohlberg's initial research and his reported longitudinal studies were with an all-male sample. Significantly, females regularly score a stage or more below males in Kohlberg's research. Gilligan also reports her research with women in the midst of real, not hypothetical, moral decisions. Based on it she asserts that the structural-developmental theory of moral reasoning is partially sound but needs correcting in its over-emphasis on justice. She finds that women are as concerned about the effects of their moral decisions on relationships as they are about justice. She asserts that the theory must be adjusted to include the voice of women in understanding moral reasoning.

Gilligan's research does not support the stereotypical understanding of men as more objective and women as more subjective. Instead, it calls us to take seriously the fact that God created humankind as both female and male and that any adequate understanding of morality or of any other aspect of human development must take into account the complementary natures of male and female. The issues of moral reasoning and identity must be "enlarged by the inclusion of responsibility and care in relationships."[8]

Robert Kegan

Robert Kegan's work is also an expansion and revision of Kohlberg. In *The Evolving Self*, Kegan develops a stage theory of

6. Robert L. Selman, *The Growth of Interpersonal Understanding: Developmental and Clinical Analysis* (New York: Academic, Developmental Psychology Series, 1980).

7. Carol Gilligan, *In a Different Voice: Psychological Theory and Women's Development* (Cambridge: Harvard University Press, 1982).

8. Ibid., p. 173.

selfhood.[9] His theory pushes the structural-developmental theory in the direction of ego development and personality theory. A significant contribution of his theory is his attempt to move from an emphasis on the stages to the process of human development. He speaks in terms not of stages but of "evolutionary truces."

Jane Loevinger

Jane Loevinger's work on ego development also follows the structural-developmental paradigm.[10] For Loevinger, ego is the central part of the self. The "ego provides the frame of reference that structures one's world and within which one perceives the world. . . ."[11] Loevinger has attempted to develop a broad approach by understanding the self as a multifaceted phenomenon, yet she remains true to the primary tenets of structural-developmental theories. She speaks of the structures of self and ego. She understands persons to interact with their environments in that they both select what stimuli they will respond to and choose a response that represents their structural frame of reference.

Loevinger posits an eight-stage theory with two transitional levels. The stages operate under the same rules as do all structural theories in that they are invariantly sequenced and hierarchical. This also implies that someone could fixate at a particular stage. The descriptions of the stages reflect Loevinger's attempt to take into account all domain areas that shape the ego. The descriptions speak to how an individual understands self and others in a growingly complex fashion. People begin with a presocial stage that reflects the undifferentiated nature of the infant, then move through the symbiotic, impulsive, self-protective, conformist, self-awareness, conscientious, individualistic, autonomous, and integrated stages. The strength of her theory rests in its attempt to incorporate the many dimensions of development into an overall scheme. Its weakness rests in its excessive loyalty to the structural-developmental paradigm.

William Perry

One final structural theory to be described was developed by William Perry.[12] Perry began his work "innocently" in that he did

9. Robert Kegan, *The Evolving Self: Problem and Process in Human Development* (Cambridge: Harvard University Press, 1982).

10. Jane Loevinger, *Ego Development: Conceptions and Theories* (San Francisco: Jossey-Bass, 1976).

11. Ibid., pp. 9, 10.

12. William G. Perry, *Forms of Intellectual and Ethical Development in the College Years* (New York: Holt, Rinehart and Winston, 1970).

not assume a structural-developmental paradigm. He arrived at the structural aspects as he attempted to make sense of data he gathered on college students. He was interested in the common problems students had when he spoke with them at the counseling center at Harvard University. From this he developed a longitudinal research project that served as the basis for his theory. The theory describes college students as beginning at a dualistic level in their view of truth, life, and authority. They see everything in black-and-white or right-and-wrong categories. From here they move to a multiplistic level at which they view all truth and authority as basically relative. They are unable to apply critical judgment to ideas or to assess them logically. The final level is relativism, in which persons realize the relative nature of much of our knowledge but can assess competing claims critically and commit themselves to an opinion. Within each of these levels there are several positions through which persons develop.

Notice that Perry intentionally avoids the language of stages because he does not affirm all of the basic tenets of structural theories. He finds that some people may retreat, temporarize, or escape from the developmental pattern. This represents some difference from structural theories in that it acknowledges the possibility of something like regression. He also attempts to take into account the affective dimension of development as he speaks of the courage and grief required to give up a dualistic world view. His theory has received much attention from both student development personnel and college faculties because of its help in understanding college students. There is much here yet to be mined for Christian formation.

Critique of Structural Theories

These three final theories lead to a discussion of functional developmental theories. Kegan, Loevinger, and Perry acknowledge the need for a theory that takes into account the affective domain. Perry at least entertains the possibility that regression may occur in development. A critique of structural-developmental theories, however, is in order.

Structural-developmental theories preserve high regard for the person. They do not inherently advocate a high view of the person, but they are compatible with it. Persons are seen not as mere reactors to environmental stimuli but as active agents in the process of development. The theories do not understand persons romantically but recognize that they are affected by environmental factors.

These theories are generally compatible with a Christian world view. However, one problem that seems inherent in structural theories is their tendency toward relativism. Both Kohlberg's and Perry's theories challenge all approaches to life that claim to have some apprehension of the facts and issues. One must be careful not to affirm these theories too easily before considering their impact on one's own perception of faith. I find the theories useful at this point because, as Paul says, "for now we see in a mirror, dimly" (1 Cor. 13:12). This warns us to realize the tentativeness of our apprehension of truth and that we do not have complete knowledge.

Finally, these theories are very useful in understanding Christian formation and, in particular, education for Christian formation. Much has been done with them in education, including religious education, because they enable us to understand the processes that lead to development and learning.

Functional Theories

As has been pointed out before, functional stage theories differ from structural stage theories. In functional theory, the "question is not whether but how one progresses through the appointed stages."[13] Persons will encounter each psychosocial stage; the question is how well they will deal with the issues present in each stage. Another important quality of functional stage theory is that the stages are cumulative. That is, if the resolution of a particular psychosocial crisis is positive, then that strength will be carried forward; if the resolution is negative, then the resulting weakness will be carried forward. Several theories illustrate these general principles, but Erik Erikson's is central.

Erik Erikson

Erikson has become something of a legend in his own time. He began his psychological work with Freud and worked in child therapy for many years. He was with Freud in Vienna for fifteen years before coming to America, where he continued clinical work as well as teaching at Harvard. His first book, *Childhood and Society*,

13. Donald Capps, *Life Cycle Theory and Pastoral Care* (Philadelphia: Fortress, 1983).

included the first articulation of his eight-stage theory of the human life cycle. Since then he has written many books and articles based on his research and clinical practice.[14] We turn now to several of the major emphases of his theory.

Erikson's theory begins with the epigenetic principle. In biological usage, this refers to the inherent pattern manifested in the development of an embryo. For Erikson, it implies that the psychosocial development of individuals follows a ground plan inherent to humans. It is not a deterministic idea, because the resolution of each stage is open, but it does imply that each stage arises at its point of ascendancy. It also implies that each stage is related to all other stages. This is exemplified by the idea that a positive resolution of one stage contributes to a positive resolution of the following stages. It also affirms that each stage exists in some form prior to its point of ascendancy. The issue of intimacy, therefore, which is ascendant during young adulthood, also exists in some form prior to young adulthood.

A second emphasis is interactionism, the belief that people's development is not simply the result of genetic endowment on one side or environmental shaping on the other but is carried forward by both nature and nurture. Erikson speaks of the interaction of "psyche, soma, and ethos." By this he asserts that the psyche, or the accrued ego of the individual, contributes to development, as do the soma, or body, and the ethos, which consists of culture, society, and historical moment. The interaction of these components gives rise to the development of the individual.

Finally there are the stages in Erikson's theory. Erikson's stages are bipolar. Each stage has a positive aspect and a negative aspect. Many people assume that Erikson asserts that these stages should be resolved completely to the positive side of the polarities, but this is not what Erikson advocates. For Erikson, "what counts is the ratio between the positive and negative poles."[15]

A wonderful film, *Everyone Rides the Carousel*, artistically explains Erikson's theory. In the account of the first stage in Erikson's theory, which is trust versus mistrust, the producers of the film depict his concern for proper ratio. Infants must learn that their caretakers and they themselves are trustworthy. At one point in the movie the infant encounters steep basement stairs and considers exploring them. The symbol for mistrust appears, warning the infant that this is not a

14. For a good biography of Erikson, see Robert Coles, *Erik Erikson* (New York: DaCapo, 1970).
15. Capps, *Life Cycle Theory*, p. 22.

good thing. The point is that some things should be mistrusted, and we must maintain some sense of mistrust in order to survive. Erikson hopes that the ratio is predominantly to the positive, but he acknowledges the necessity of a minimal level of the negative pole of each stage.

The film also depicts two other important notions embedded in Erikson's stage theory. First, there seems to be a cycling process involved in the theory, which explains Erikson's continual use of the phrase *life cycle*. The issue of trust, which begins the life cycle, reappears in the last stage. Trust, or faith, is part of the resolution of the last stage. Thus, Erikson seems to entertain a cyclical notion of life. Second, since the individual cannot literally recycle, the idea of cycles is found in what Erikson calls the "cogwheeling of generations." This implies that each generation of individuals is connected with both the preceding and the following generations. This is an important notion to help us remember that each person's development is intertwined with the development of his forebears and his descendants. What is also implicit here, and is made explicit by Erikson, is that the "historical moment" when one encounters a crisis will also influence the resolution of that crisis.

I will not discuss each of the stages in depth at this point but will briefly discuss three aspects of each stage. First, each includes its own actual psychosocial crisis. This is the issue that individuals face at particular points in their lives. According to Erikson, persons encounter the following eight crises: (1) infancy: trust versus mistrust; (2) toddlerhood: autonomy versus shame and doubt; (3) preschool: initiative versus guilt; (4) school age: industry versus inferiority; (5) adolescence: identity versus identity confusion; (6) young adulthood: intimacy versus isolation; (7) middle adulthood: generativity versus self-absorption; and (8) later adulthood: integrity versus despair.

Second, each stage includes what Erikson first called ego strengths but later called virtues. These are strengths of the individual that arise with the healthy resolution of each stage. Like the crises, these virtues also include the negative side, which Erikson calls antipathies, or which we might call vices.[16] Beginning with infancy these are: hope versus withdrawal; will versus compulsion; purpose versus inhibition; competence versus inertia; fidelity versus repudiation; love versus exclusivity; care versus rejectivity; and wisdom versus disdain.

Third, each stage includes what Erikson calls a ritualization. Ritu-

16. See Donald Capps, *Deadly Sins and Saving Virtues* (Philadelphia: Fortress, 1987).

alization consists of ways in which individuals interact or socialize with those around them. They are the familiar patterns of human interaction that allow us to be with others. On the negative side are ritualisms, which are unhealthy expressions of the normal ways of interaction. Beginning at infancy the ritualizations and ritualisms are: numinous versus idolism; judicious versus legalism; dramatic versus moralism; formal versus formalism; ideological versus totalism; affiliative versus elitism; generational versus authoritism; and integral versus dogmatism. There is much to explain in each of these aspects of the stages, and we will do that later when we treat Erikson's theory as a primary framework for a theory of Christian formation.

Daniel Levinson, George Vaillant, and Robert Havighurst

Although not as clearly associated as are the structural-developmentalists, several other theorists operate from a primarily functionalist perspective. Most who do so have not developed a schedule of stages or cycles, but they do think of the life cycle in terms of Erikson's theory. An exception to this is some recent work in adult development represented by Daniel Levinson's *The Seasons of a Man's Life*,[17] in which Levinson describes periods of development in adult life. Another who follows closely after the functional theory of Erikson in the study of adult life is George Vaillant. In *Adaptation to Life*, Vaillant describes his longitudinal research with men, which he believes corroborates, with some revision, Erikson's work on adulthood.[18] Robert Havighurst's developmental task approach is also functionalist and describes a schedule of developmental tasks that arise across the life cycle.[19] Havighurst asserts that these tasks come about as the result of one or all of three factors: physiological growth (walking becomes a developmental task at the point when the child's body is prepared to deal with it), cultural expectations (starting formal schooling or learning to drive), and personal aspirations (inner desires and drives that motivate persons to develop; an example is individuals' setting high goals for themselves). Most developmental tasks arise as a complex interaction of all of these, which is why Hav-

17. Daniel J. Levinson, et al., *The Seasons of a Man's Life* (New York: Ballantine, 1978).

18. George E. Vaillant, *Adaptation to Life* (Boston: Little, Brown, 1977).

19. Robert J. Havighurst, *Developmental Tasks and Education* (New York: Longman, 1972). See also Robert J. Havighurst, *The Educational Mission of the Church* (Philadelphia: Westminster, 1965).

ighurst can be understood as working from the functionalist perspective. Another important concept to be gleaned from Havighurst's work is that of the teachable moment: "When the body is ripe, and society requires, and the self is ready to achieve a certain task, the teachable moment has come."[20] This is an important concept in a developmental approach to education.

James Marcia

Several others belong to the functionalist family, although they do not develop stage theories. James Marcia has contributed to an understanding of Erikson's fifth stage, "identity versus identity confusion," by developing an instrument to assess where an individual is in the process of identity formation.[21] Marcia delineates four identity statuses that are typical of adolescents negotiating this crisis. More will be said about Marcia when we discuss adolescence in particular. His contribution to functional developmental theory has been very useful.

Robert Coles

Robert Coles also works from a broad functional developmental perspective.[22] Coles has written what most consider to be the finest biography and description of Erik Erikson's life and work. His work with children has been greatly influenced by Erikson's theoretical assumptions.

David Elkind

Finally, David Elkind must be mentioned.[23] Some consider Elkind as influenced mainly by structural-developmental theory, but his work crosses the technical boundary between the two developmental approaches, and he is one of America's finest interpreters of Piaget. His latest book concentrates mostly on Erikson's theory.[24] Elkind's

20. Havighurst, *Developmental Tasks*, p. 7.

21. For a good summary of James Marcia's work, see Rolf Muuss, *Theories of Adolescence*, 3d ed. (New York: Random House, 1982), chapter 4.

22. See Robert Coles, *Erik Erikson*, and *The Moral Life of Children* (Boston: Houghton Mifflin, 1986), and "The Faith of Children," *Sojourners* 11(May 1982), pp. 12–16.

23. See David Elkind, *The Hurried Child: Growing Up Too Fast Too Soon* (New York: Addison-Wesley, 1981), *All Grown Up and No Place to Go: Teenagers in Crisis* (New York: Addison-Wesley, 1984), and *Miseducation: Preschoolers at Risk* (New York: Alfred A. Knopf, 1987).

24. Elkind, *Miseducation*.

early research includes much on the religious thinking of children. His later and more general writings have been on the effects of hurrying children and adolescents in their development. These books are some of the best at presenting an integrated perspective of developmental theory and making the issues understandable and useful for parents and educators alike.

Assessment of Developmental Theory

A Superior Approach

We have been reviewing the theories of human development according to four criteria, the first of which is whether the theory preserves the importance of personhood. On this criterion developmental theory does well. Developmental theory approaches human growth from the perspective of healthy development and assumes that something like the person or self does exist. It describes the general patterns of development that all healthy persons exhibit. Each developmental approach assumes that a real self develops. Most approaches assume that persons are at least co-responsible for their development, and these theories assume an interactionist approach to development. Developmental theories recognize the complexity of human development in interaction with family, society, and self.

The second criterion is the theory's compatibility with a Christian world view. The amount of interest in developmental theory in the past few years by religionists lends some support to this compatibility.

The third criterion is usefulness. Again, developmental theory does well on this criterion. For years education has used ideas such as readiness and cognitive stages. This is also true of religious education; we will soon look at a large amount of theorizing about a developmental approach to spiritual development. Developmental theory has also gained much attention from both professional therapists and lay persons who are attempting to sort out the complexity of their lives. The popularity of Gail Sheehy's *Passages* is evidence of this level of usefulness.

The fourth is usefulness for education. Clearly developmental theories have found a hungry audience among educators and the theories have stimulated valuable changes in education.

In summary, we will adopt a developmental view of human growth due to its ability to assimilate aspects of the major psychological theories and its positive outcome in regard to the four criteria.

Rationale for Its Supremacy

Before describing some of the approaches to spiritual development based on developmental theory, we need to say more about why developmental psychology is the most helpful approach to human development. Not only is it closest to our theological view of human growth, but beyond that, the processes of development that it describes tend to be most illuminating as to the actual ways in which people grow. This is not to emphasize stages. (In fact, I am skeptical of the structural theories, which tend to be overly concerned with stages rather than with people.) Rather, I want to call attention to how helpful are developmental theory's descriptions of the processes by which we understand development. Following is a summary of those that are most useful.

In developmental theory, the process of human growth is not understood as simply living out what is already there at birth. This old theory was called the homunculist theory. It postulated that individuals change little after conception. They were understood to be fully formed in the sperm or ovum. Developmental theory is more what may be called evolutionary. It views growth as development from less complex to more complex. Levels of awareness, amounts of knowledge, and abilities to act on one's environment all increase as individuals develop. With this increased complexity also comes increased differentiation. Individuals' behaviors and attitudes become more distinct from one another, and individuals themselves become more distinct from others. With the evolution of the self also comes what Piaget called decentration. The individual becomes less preoccupied with self as healthy development occurs. This growth leads to increased levels of autonomy: individuals should become less dependent on others and more self-dependent as healthy development transpires. It is important to note, however, that development is not understood in a linear fashion or as accumulative in nature. Development is not an ever-increasing amount of growth that occurs in a steady, continuous fashion. It may do so, but development is also discontinuous and irregular. It may take place but also it may not. It is not some easily predicted pattern that can be imposed on every person. It is complex and idiosyncratic, shaped by individuals' unique encounters with life and their attempts to make sense out of it.

Two major themes describe how development takes place according to developmental theory. The first of these could be called the hermeneutical process. Life is a hermeneutical question, meaning that we spend our lives attempting to make sense out of our existence. This process of making sense includes thinking, feeling, and acting. According to structural theory, growth takes place by way of dissonance. That is, in our encounters with new information and situations that put us off balance, we attempt to understand these situations in order to resolve the dissonance. Dissonance produces growth when it is within the limits of the person's psychic strength to deal with it, but it may paralyze if it is too strong. This can also be understood as the view that growth takes place through crises. One must be careful not to associate crises with only very upsetting situations. Crises, in the Eriksonian sense, are turning points or points of decision that can result in growth or stagnation.

The second theme of the process is interaction. Developmental theory does not assert that growth simply occurs naturally as individuals assert themselves; neither does it imply that growth results from environmental impact alone. Developmental theory holds that development occurs as individuals interact with the environment. Growth results from heredity plus environment plus "more." Erikson's notion of psyche captures the "more." Psyche is a difficult dimension to describe. We may understand it as personal aspirations, as does Havighurst. It is the power of the self that motivates us to grow. As Christians, we could view it as a part of the image of God in us. It is the breath of God that makes us persons and gives us these aspirations. However we understand it, developmental theory holds that growth occurs as a result of the interaction of self and environment; in that interaction, aspects of the self come together—sometimes smoothly, sometimes roughly.

Finally, there is the sense of human development. That is, as you view the entire landscape of human development, what picture do you get? Fowler calls this idea "myths of becoming."[25] This implies the narrative quality of life. That is, growth is best understood as an unfolding story and makes sense only when seen in this light. Also, a part of the sense of human development is a vision of maturity. The word *maturity* has fallen into disuse lately with our excessive concern for relativism, but it is time to recapture it in an appropriate manner. *Relativism* refers to our cultural fears of judging anyone's life by any particular standards. The word *maturity* came to mean a

25. Fowler, *Becoming Adult, Becoming Christian*.

set of narrowly prescribed behaviors that people exhibited when they became mature. It was a stagnant, suffocating notion.

Yet we threw the baby out with the bath water. We need some sense of what successful adult life looks and feels like. We need some sense of what a responsible individual feels, does, and thinks, and of how she goes about that process. Developmental theory gives us an appropriate definition or vision of maturity. Maturity is not some end point or achievement but an ever-moving target. It is a process in which there are markers that indicate that growth is occurring, but the process also keeps drawing us to more adequate ways of living. Maturity can be understood as openness to growth. William Bouwsma argues that sin is closing oneself to growth.[26] Part of maturity, in this view, is tolerance of ambiguity. If the goal of maturity is continual growth and an openness to it, then the ambiguities of life are tolerable. "I know who I am today but don't ask me about tomorrow." There needs to be a certain tentativeness in maturity. More will be added later to this when we bring theology and psychology together to address Christian maturity. Let it suffice to say here that developmental theory is compelling in part because of its vision of maturity.

The process of development as understood by developmental theory includes an evolutionary idea, an understanding of growth, and a sense of what it means to be mature. These issues, combined with the above analysis of the approach according to the four criteria applied to each psychological theory considered, indicate that developmental theory is useful in understanding the human side of Christian formation.

---

26. William Bouwsma, "Christian Adulthood," in Erik H. Erikson, ed., *Adulthood* (New York: Norton, 1978).

7

Developmental Psychology and Christian Formation

Many people have used developmental theory in their efforts to understand spiritual development. This section reviews the attempts that are most direct in their use of developmental theory and have been most influential. The discussion divides the approaches according to their primary developmental emphases: structural-developmental, functional-developmental, and integrative. The final category includes those who have worked from both structural and functional approaches as well as those who have worked from a more theological position. The order of each section follows the historical development of the approach, although this is sometimes difficult to ascertain.

Structural Theories

Ronald Goldman

Ronald Goldman is one of the pioneers in the study of religious development from a developmental psychological position. His work is found primarily in *Religious Thinking from Childhood to Adolescence* and *Readiness for Religion*.[1] Goldman interviewed about thirty children in England in the early 1960s. He investigated whether the

1. Ronald Goldman, *Religious Thinking from Childhood to Adolescence* (New York: Seabury, 1964), and *Readiness for Religion* (New York: Seabury, 1965).

Piagetian stages of cognitive development held true for the religious domain. He concluded that they do and proceeded to describe three stages of religious development based on his research. Pre-school children were described as intuitive in their religious thinking. Five-to nine-year-olds view God in physical or anthropomorphic terms, giving God a body that typically is old and bearded. From ages nine to thirteen, children think concretely about God, to understand him in more logical and concrete ways. Adolescents thirteen and older begin to apply early formal operations to their religious thinking. This results in four problems: the question of literalism and author-itism, a two-world view, Old Testament primitivism, and biblical relevance.[2] Goldman also addressed religious education for these stages. He felt that during the first stage education should be experience oriented, in the second stage it should concentrate on the facts of religion, and in the third stage it should deal with great themes of religion, not details. Goldman's work has been foundational. One must, however, be careful to recognize the implicit theological bias in his work. Goldman seems to have difficulty in holding to any literal sense of some Old Testament events. This does not imply that these passages should or should not be considered literally, but one readily sees how theology imposes itself on psychology and vice versa.

David Elkind

David Elkind addresses religious development in children by describing the roots of religious thinking.[3] In his earliest work on religious thinking Elkind described the prayer life of children, illustrating how they tend to move from more self-centered prayer to prayer for others. He also contributed a substantial chapter on religious thinking in children and adolescents in Strommen's seminal book on religious development.[4] Elkind has more recently become an important figure in the public's eye with his books *The Hurried Child, All Grown Up with No Place to Go*, and *Miseducation*.[5] In each

2. Goldman, *Religious Thinking*, pp. 242–45.

3. David Elkind, *The Child and Society* (New York: Oxford, 1979).

4. Merton P. Strommen, ed., *Research on Religious Development: A Comprehensive Handbook* (New York: Hawthorn, 1971).

5. David Elkind, *The Hurried Child: Growing Up Too Fast Too Soon* (New York: Addison-Wesley, 1981), All Grown Up and No Place to Go: Teenagers in Crisis (New York: Addison-Wesley, 1984), and Miseducation: Preschoolers at Risk (New York: Alfred A. Knopf, 1987).

of these Elkind urges parents not to push their children toward early "success" in school, athletics, or whatever parents think is important. Throughout these books Elkind shows his sensitivity to and desire for the religious element in the lives of children and adolescents.

James Fowler

James Fowler has made the structural-developmental approach to faith a common and compelling idea. Fowler comes to the study of faith development out of his early work with a retreat center called Interpreter's House. There Fowler began to observe the life stories of people who came to the center, and there he began to read Erik Erikson. After some time at Interpreter's House, Fowler went to Harvard Divinity School to do doctoral work, writing his dissertation on the theology of H. Richard Niebuhr.[6] He began to teach at Harvard and there encountered the work of Lawrence Kohlberg. Being taken by structuralism in relation to his concerns for the development of faith, Fowler began his early research. He first reported his stages of faith in *Life Maps*, co-authored with Sam Keen. The research received immediate attention and several books soon followed. In 1981, *Stages of Faith* was published, which reported fully the theoretical background of the research and its results. This was followed in 1984 by *Becoming Adult, Becoming Christian*, and in 1987 by *Faith Development and Pastoral Care.*[7]

Fowler's work has drawn much attention and generated much thought and work in the area of faith development. The attention is both supportive and critical, with concerns about both its psychological and its theological bases. We now turn to the theoretical assumptions of Fowler's approach, describe the stages of faith development, and then address a few concerns about the approach.

The theory is clearly a structural-developmental approach. It investigates and describes the ways in which people think about faith, not what they believe. The allegiance to structuralism is also clear in the description of the six stages of faith, which closely resemble Kohlberg's six stages of moral development.

6. See James W. Fowler, *To See the Kingdom: The Theological Vision of H. Richard Niebuhr* (Boston: University Press of America, 1974).

7. See James W. Fowler and Sam Keen, *Life Maps: Conversations on the Journey of Faith*, ed. Jerome Berryman (Waco: Word, 1981); Fowler, Stages of Faith: The Psychology of Human Development and the Quest for Faith (New York: Harper & Row, 1984); Fowler, Becoming Adult, Becoming Christian (New York: Harper & Row, 1987); and Fowler, Faith Development and Pastoral Care (Philadelphia: Fortress, 1987).

Fowler's definition of faith also must be made clear. He assumes that faith is "the most fundamental category in the human quest for relation to transcendence."[8] By this he implies that faith is something that all human beings have. Fowler also states that "faith is an orientation of the total person. . . ."[9] He emphasizes that faith is not separated from the rest of an individual's life but is intricately related to the whole person. For Fowler, "faith is a relational enterprise. . . ."[10] The relationship is threefold: self, others, and "center of value and power" or, more directly, God. It is the mix of these three that begins to bring about a coherent definition of faith. "Faith forms a way of seeing our everyday life. . . ."[11] This is, in essence, what Fowler means by faith. It is a way of seeing the world and making sense out of our existence.

Fowler identifies six stages of faith:

Stage 0: Primal or Undifferentiated Faith. Fowler calls this a pre-stage and finds it in pre-birth and infancy. This stage revolves around the infant's development of trust in the environment and the self. Here our earliest concept of God occurs.

Stage 1: Intuitive-Projective Faith. This stage includes the ages of about four to seven. (Remember, however, that structural theory is not tied to chronology but only approximates the ages in which the stages typically occur.) Children in this stage think preoperationally and think of faith in terms of magic and fantasy. They also take on the faith of their parents.

Stage 2: Mythic-Literal Faith. Children aged seven to eleven tend to operate with concrete operational thought. This leads to an appropriation of faith and beliefs in a very literalistic fashion. Children also begin to appreciate the power of story, and narrative becomes an important means by which they make sense of themselves.

Stage 3: Synthetic-Conventional Faith. In the pre-teen and early teen years, around eleven to thirteen, adolescents begin to use formal operations in their cognition. Young adolescents attempt to synthesize the various threads that make up their lives and weave them into something coherent. They do this by making use of the most conventional forms of faith prevalent in their particular subculture. For this reason this stage can be named "Faith as Conformity." Chil-

8. Fowler, *Stages of Faith*, p. 17.
9. Ibid., p. 17.
10. Ibid., p. 18.
11. Ibid., p. 24.

dren are greatly influenced by peers and attractive authority figures as they attempt to create their own faith.

Stage 4: Individuative-Reflective Faith. Young adults may (but will not necessarily) begin to move into this stage of faith. It is a stage of attempting to truly own one's faith. It is individuative in that young adults must now deal with the explicit creation of their own sense of self and faith. It is reflective in that they can now stand back and critically reflect on the influences that have shaped them thus far. Doubting, questioning, and rejecting traditional beliefs are common to this stage.

Stage 5: Conjunctive Faith. This stage may be called "Faith as Paradox" because of its attempt to relax the earlier attempts to resolve all of the problems or paradoxes of faith. It is often not found before age thirty, if then. The most obvious characteristics of the stage are the willingness to live with paradox and tension in one's faith and a new sense of simplicity in faith. Persons discover anew the richness of symbol and mystery. This should not be confused with a return to a simplistic faith but is only constructed after the hard intellectual work of previous stages.

Stage 6: Universalizing Faith. Fowler does not see this stage being arrived at before the mid-life years, and rarely there. In it persons totally give up themselves. Fowler would consider people like Mother Teresa, Deitrich Bonhoeffer, and Martin Luther King, Jr., to be living in stage 6.

These are brief, concise summaries of faith stages. They could be expanded, but they capture the essential nature of each of Fowler's stages. We will now address a few concerns about Fowler's theory.

First, there are problems in the qualitative research methodology used in faith development research, problems that apply to any developmental research. The semi-clinical interview lends itself to some difficulties when one attempts to gather a large body of data that must be analyzed according to a guiding theory. The research is vulnerable to the problems of inter-rater variability and researcher bias. Inter-rater variability is the tendency of different raters to give different scores to the same data. Researcher bias is the tendency of interviewers to be overly subjective in data collection and reporting. It is easy to become sympathetic or unsympathetic with subjects, thus yielding scores that are skewed. The developmental stage of the researcher may itself influence the reporting and scoring of data. Data may also suffer from retrospective reporting of significant events by subjects. They may reinterpret past events in ways that make them more or less meaningful than they were when they occurred. It may be argued that this does not affect the current stage of subjects and, therefore, is not a problem. Not so. It does reflect the possibility of self-deception in all persons that will obviously affect any research.

Second, there is the problem of ideological bias. This takes several directions, the first being the problem of beginning with a particular theoretical stance. As C. Ellis Nelson and D. Aleshire state, "The data have been collected according to a stage theory of human development."[12] If you begin by assuming a structural stage theory, that is what you will find. If a more Eriksonian approach had been assumed, the results would have looked different. There is also a cultural problem inherent in the theory. According to John Broughton, "Faith development theory has its intellectual origins in the American functionalist, pragmatist, and symbolic interactionist traditions."[13] This implies a particular cultural view that colors the theory. This is evident in the problem of language. Researchers tend to give higher scores to subjects who are articulate and educated than to those who are not. Ideological bias also arises because of Fowler's attempt to create a broad, generic theory. Again Broughton states, "The theorist's desire for universality has eventuated in an intolerance of specificity."[14] In some sense this forces the theory to settle for the lowest common denominator, which strips faith of some of its most important aspects.

Third, there are theological problems in Fowler's theory. The desire for universality leads to a broad definition of faith as a world view and an almost exclusive focus on structural dimensions to the exclusion of how specific content might shape people's faith. Craig Dykstra has shown how a more explicit theological definition of faith brings about a different theory of faith development.[15] Fowler's theory shows some on theological bias. By placing a type of theological universalism at stage 6, Fowler exhibits a vision of mature faith that is informed by the liberal Christian theological tradition. Those of more conservative theological traditions have difficulty

12. C. Ellis Nelson and D. Aleshire, "Research in Faith Development," in *Faith Development and Fowler*, ed. Craig Dykstra and Sharon Parks (Birmingham, Ala.: Religious Education Press, 1986), p. 186.

13. John Broughton, "The Political Psychology of Faith Development Theory," in *Faith Development and Fowler*, ed. Dykstra and Parks, p. 90.

14. Ibid., p. 107.

15. Craig Dykstra, "What Is Faith? An Experiment in the Hypothetical Mode," in *Faith Development and Fowler*, ed. Dykstra and Parks, pp. 45–64.

accepting stage 6 as a vision of mature faith. What is interesting, however, is their acceptance of the stage sequence up to about stage 4 or 5, then their rejection of stage 6. While the more conservative traditions do not find the theory specific enough in theological content, some from less conservative traditions find it overly specific.

Mary Wilcox

Mary Wilcox's book *Developmental Journey* grows out of a predominantly Kohlbergian framework that she uses to address faith.[16] She has also done her own research in this domain, and she incorporates into her work some of Fowler's early findings. The major contributions of her work are, first, her early attempts to understand religious development from the developmental psychological approach, and, second, her useful discussions of teaching for religious and moral growth. The book is practical and insightful.

Bruce Powers

Bruce Powers's *Growing Faith* is a practical book that outlines five phases of faith and discusses how faith develops and can be nourished. He bases his phases on interviews with about six hundred people. In the analysis of these interviews he describes the five phases of faith. He then attempts to discuss his ideas in the light of Fowler's stages and the styles of faith identified by John Westerhoff. Powers's work is insightful and highly useful, helping us to understand faith as a process and how to facilitate its growth in ourselves and others.[17]

Sharon Parks

Sharon Parks's *The Critical Years* is a significant work that expands Fowler's theory and addresses the higher education community.[18] Parks expands on Fowler's work by incorporating a stage that she calls "Young Adult Faith." Her research with college students led her to believe that there is a distinct stage between Fowler's stages 3 and 4. She finds in college-age persons and those in the young adult years a form of faith that is very different from synthetic-

16. Mary M. Wilcox, *Developmental Journey: A Guide to the Development of Logical and Moral Reasoning and Social Perspective* (Nashville: Abingdon, 1979).

17. Bruce P. Powers, *Growing Faith* (Nashville: Broadman, 1982).

18. Sharon Parks, *The Critical Years* (New York: Harper & Row, 1986).

conventional faith primarily because of the presence of true critical thinking, yet is also different from individuative-reflective faith due to its exploratory nature and its fragile dependence on the self. Her contribution to the higher education community is important, particularly as she speaks of the need for vision and mentoring to assist students in developing faith. Her work does little to change in any way the primary understandings of Fowler's approach. It is also important to point out that she is not addressing Christian higher education but is using faith in its generic sense, which diminishes the explicit usefulness of her work in overtly Christian settings.

Functional Theories

Lewis Sherrill

One of the earliest attempts to speak to spiritual development from a functional developmental approach is Lewis Sherrill's *The Struggle of the Soul*.[19] Sherrill addresses how people encounter God in the various stages of human development. He thinks of faith not as just another aspect of the developing person but as something that interacts with the various stages of life. He begins by speaking to three ways in which we can look at life: as treadmill, saga, or pilgrimage. This discussion is helpful in that he integrates biblical notions of human growth with psychological notions to affirm a particular way of perceiving human development. The remainder of the book moves through the life cycle from early childhood to old age and discusses the psychological issues of each and how faith interacts with each. Although Sherrill does not explicitly mention it, he clearly is informed by Erikson's work.

John Gleason

In 1975 John Gleason wrote *Growing Up to God*, in which he sought to describe a developmental psychology of religion.[20] Gleason is a clinical psychologist and works primarily from a clinical perspective. He begins with Erikson's eight stages of the life cycle and then places a "religious overlay" on each stage. His basic assumption

19. Lewis Sherrill, *The Struggle of the Soul* (New York: Macmillan, 1954).
20. John J. Gleason, Jr., *Growing Up to God: Eight Steps in Religious Development* (Nashville: Abingdon, 1975).

is that particular theological doctrines are in focus at particular stages of human development and that the way a particular theological lesson is learned has either positive or negative effects on our future religious development. Gleason's major contribution is in assisting us to reflect on the theological themes that may be a part of each of the life stages. Following is the scheme he proposes:

Stage 1: Basic Trust and the Doctrine of God
Stage 2: Autonomy and Good and Evil
Stage 3: Initiative and Sin and Redemption
Stage 4: Industry and Works
Stage 5: Identity and Man (doctrine of humankind)
Stage 6: Intimacy and Christology
Stage 7: Generativity and Creation
Stage 8: Integrity and Eschatology

Gleason's work has not received much attention, but it is important especially as we try to keep the idea of practical theology in mind, that is, our attempt to integrate psychology and theology for ministry.

Donald Capps

Donald Capps is one of the best interpreters of Erikson's theory and its application to religion and, in particular, pastoral counseling, on which he has written several books. Three of these are useful for Christian formation. In *Pastoral Care*, Capps develops a thematic approach to the subject. He uses the theories of several psychologists, especially Erikson. He sees Erikson as presenting themes of human growth that are both age-period specific and perennial. He defines themes as "the basic personal interests or intentions that direct an individual's life."[21] Capps recognizes the compatibility of the theological themes with particular Eriksonian stages and develops these together. Following is his proposal:

Stage 1: Providence and Trust versus Mistrust
Stage 2: Grace or Gratefulness and Autonomy versus Shame and Doubt

21. Donald Capps, *Pastoral Care: A Thematic Approach* (Philadelphia: Fortress, 1983), p. 18.

Stage 3: Repentance and Initiative versus Guilt
Stage 4: Vocation and Industry versus Inferiority
Stage 5: Faith and Identity versus Identity Confusion
Stage 6: Communion and Intimacy versus Isolation
Stage 7: Vocation and Generativity versus Stagnation
Stage 8: Awareness of the Holy and Integrity versus Despair[22]

Two other books by Capps deserve mention here. In *Life Cycle Theory and Pastoral Care*,[23] Capps develops the idea that a pastor is both a moral counselor and a ritual coordinator. First he describes Erikson's schedule of virtues and how they assist one in understanding the moral nature of the life cycle. Then he uses Erikson's idea of ritualizations across the life cycle and traces their implications for the pastor in coordinating rituals of faith life. His brief introduction to Erikson's theory is one of the finest available. In *Deadly Sins and Saving Virtues*,[24] Capps further develops Erikson's idea of the virtues by speaking to their respective vices. This provocative book is an important contribution to the study of religion from an Eriksonian perspective.

Several other works are significant for the study of Christian formation from a functional developmental perspective. Evelyn and James Whitehead's *Christian Life Patterns* speaks to the relationship of spiritual growth and adult development.[25] The Whiteheads discuss research current when they wrote that was working toward a developmental understanding of adulthood; then they use Erikson's adult stages as a lens through which to view adult spiritual growth. Their book is among the first of many to address adult development and spirituality.

Also in the area of adulthood is the research directed by Kenneth Stokes for the Religious Education Association's project "Faith Development in the Adult Life Cycle." The project began with a set of hypotheses generated by discussion of both functional and structural approaches to adult development. These hypotheses were tested

22. Ibid., pp. 113–15.
23. Donald Capps, *Life Cycle Theory and Pastoral Care* (Philadelphia: Fortress, 1983).
24. Donald Capps, *Deadly Sins and Saving Virtues* (Philadelphia: Fortress, 1987).
25. Evelyn E. Whitehead and James D. Whitehead, *Christian Life Patterns: The Psychological Challenges and Religious Invitations of Adult Life* (New York: Doubleday, 1979).

by phone interviews and in-depth interviews with a smaller sample. Using both Fowler's and Erikson's theories, Stokes analyzed the data to develop a general idea of how adults think about adult life and faith. The results have generated much interest and are being used to develop religious educational resources for adults.[26]

Integrative Approaches

John Westerhoff

Some writers have addressed spiritual development from a developmental perspective but have been more theologically oriented and less dependent on developmental psychological approaches. The first of these is John Westerhoff, who develops the idea of "styles of faithing."[27] Westerhoff asserts that faith is a verb and must be seen as active, which is why he speaks of styles of faithing. He also views the growth of faith as akin to the growth of a tree. A tree adds rings as it grows but is a tree even when it is a sapling. Also, a tree does not shed rings as it grows but adds new rings while retaining old ones. In fact, if the old rings were done away with, the tree would be hollow. So it is with faith. We have faith first in the form of experienced faith. This is faith that we assimilate from faithful others in our infancy and early childhood. We add affiliative faithing, which seeks to belong and be cared for by a community of faithing people. We exhibit a style of faith that allows us to belong. Then we add searching faith during the time of critical reflection and questioning, usually in later adolescence. Finally, we add owned faith, which attempts to bring together our professed faith with what we actually do. Again, these are tree rings that build on each other.

Craig Dykstra

Craig Dykstra addresses Christian formation in *Vision and Character*.[28] He critiques Kohlberg's approach to moral development and advocates visional morality in place of Kohlberg's juridical morality.

26. Kenneth Stokes, ed., *Faith Development in the Adult Life Cycle* (New York: Sadlier, 1982).

27. John H. Westerhoff III, *Will Our Children Have Faith?* (New York: Seabury, 1976).

28. Craig Dykstra, *Vision and Character: A Christian Educator's Alternative to Kohlberg* (Mahwah, N.J.: Paulist, 1981).

The significance of this piece is its theological critique of structural developmental theory. Dykstra has extended this critique to Fowler's theory by showing that a more explicitly theological understanding of faith would yield a different notion of how human development and faith intersect.[29]

Gabriel Moran

Gabriel Moran is also critical of the structural-developmental approaches to faith development and addresses these concerns in *Religious Education Development*.[30] He introduces developmental approaches and critiques them, then proposes his own approach from a more theological position. He treats at length the language problems of the idea of development and what the word connotes. The book is useful in gaining perspective on the study of faith development.

So ends our journey into the use of developmental theory for understanding Christian formation. The approach to Christian formation to be developed here will be a predominantly functional-developmental approach but will use structural theory where it is helpful. I hope this chapter provides a base of knowledge and understanding of why I use developmental theory as the perspective most helpful in integrating psychology and theology for Christian formation and how these theories have been used to date.

---

29. See *Faith Development and Fowler*, ed. Dykstra and Parks.
30. Gabriel Moran, *Religious Education Development* (New York and Minneapolis: Harper & Row/Winston, 1983).

Part **3**

An Integrative Approach to Christian Formation

8

Faith and Vision

We are now ready to integrate the theological and developmental psychological considerations in order to formulate an approach to Christian formation. The purpose of this chapter is to begin to articulate a practical theology of Christian formation. To accomplish this task, we will address two issues. First, we will attempt to define faith in a way that is faithful to both theological and psychological dimensions. Second, we will move toward a description of the *telos*, the goal or vision, for Christian formation. We will do this by developing a definition of maturity.

Definition of Faith

Undoubtedly the most-discussed theory of faith development is James Fowler's. But a shortcoming of the theory rests in Fowler's definition of faith. Although there is much to commend it, its essence is too psychological. Generally, Fowler defines faith as a way of being that shapes our lives as we face the realities of existence. For Fowler, all humans have faith; it is a universal aspect of human life. It need not be religious and could even be antireligious. Those who desire to incorporate theological considerations into their understanding of faith are immediately taken aback by Fowler's overly psychological definition and its theological poverty.

What does theology contribute to a definition of faith? First, it understands faith as more than human activity. Gabriel Moran states,

"Faith in its richest, most important meaning is not an object of human possession. It is a gift to which a human being responds."[1] Moran carefully preserves the dual nature of faith as human response and divine activity. Many avoid discussion of the human response side of faith, assuming that it leads to salvation by works. While we can appreciate the concern to preserve the truth that sinful persons cannot respond to God without God's initiative in reaching out to them, we must realize the weakness of this view. Its overemphasis on human inability undermines human responsibility to grow in faith. Faith is first God's activity, but it is also "appropriate and intentional participation in the redemptive activity of God."[2] Faith is human response to God's redemption. "There is no neat traceable line between God's activity and human response," writes Thomas Langford, "yet the reality of God's initiating grace and human response to it are both present."[3] Our definition of faith must underscore the specifics of Christian theological categories and communicate the truth that faith is also a human activity.

Faith as both divine initiative and human response is best understood within the categories of orthodoxy, orthopraxy, and orthopathy.[4] We are particularly interested here in discussing the human side of faith, which includes belief, behavior, and attitude. Another way to understand this threefold definition is to think in terms of cognitive, physical, and emotional aspects of human faith. These will be discussed separately, but they are interrelated aspects, none of which can stand alone as a definition of faith. Faith is not orthodoxy alone or orthopraxy alone or orthopathy alone. It is these three aspects braided together in dynamic relationship to make a strong rope.

Faith as Orthodoxy

Orthodoxy is the most cognitive aspect of faith. Christian faith must include believing correctly. Paul was most concerned with this aspect of faith. We must believe properly about God. For instance,

1. Gabriel Moran, *Religious Education Development* (New York and Minneapolis: Harper & Row/Winston, 1982), p. 122.
2. Craig Dykstra, "What Is Faith? An Experiment in the Hypothetical Mode," in *Faith Development and Fowler*, ed. Craig Dykstra and Sharon Parks (Birmingham, Ala.: Religious Education Press, 1986), p. 55.
3. Thomas Langford, *Practical Divinity: Theology in the Wesleyan Tradition* (Nashville: Abingdon, 1983), p. 32.
4. See Theodore Runyon, "Conversion—Yesterday, Today and Tomorrow," a paper presented at Minister's Week at Emory University, January 17, 1984.

we must believe truly about how God, in Christ, was reconciling the world to himself. This is why Fowler's definition of faith is insufficient. It speaks to a part of Christian faith but neglects a central aspect. Daniel Jenkins calls this part of faith the "scandalous particularity" of Christian faith. Any old belief structure will not do. Particular claims must be addressed cognitively and held as true. "Faith is not only the act of setting one's heart," writes Sharon Parks, "it is also what one sets one's heart upon."[5]

Orthodoxy, faith as belief, also includes an aspect of Fowler's definition of faith—the cognitive dimension of meaning making. We not only hold beliefs about God, we hold them in particular ways. We think about the same concept in quite different ways. Consider, for instance, the story of Nicodemus in John 3. When Jesus tells Nicodemus that in order to see the kingdom of God one must be born again, Nicodemus responds in amazement. "How can anyone be born after having grown old? Can one enter a second time into the mother's womb and be born?" We may think Nicodemus is silly to take this literally. But many children and even some adults do the same thing based on their cognitive level. Nicodemus illustrates a particular way of constructing, or making sense out of, information. Faith does have a structuring component to it. We do make sense out of knowledge and experience on the basis of our cognitive structures.

Faith as orthodoxy includes both what we believe and how we believe it—believing a particular story and making a particular sense out of it cognitively. The definition of faith here informed by theological notions is quite different from Fowler's. Walter Brueggemann, in discussing the faith of Israel, states that an insistence on a biblical understanding of faith sets it "apart from much of the conversation about faith development that attempts to be scientific and therefore substantively neutral."[6] Christian beliefs are anything but neutral.

Faith as Orthopraxy

Orthopraxy, or correct practice—the doing of meaningful, critically determined action—is a second major component of faith. As we saw in the non-Pauline corpus in particular, we are called to do as Christ would have us do. Or, as Jesus himself states, "If you love me,

5. Sharon Parks, *The Critical Years* (New York: Harper & Row, 1986), p. 26.
6. Walter Brueggemann, *Hope Within History* (Atlanta: John Knox, 1987), p. 7.

you will keep my commandments" (John 14:15). We are not called to simplistic activism undetermined by critical thought. Instead, the action God calls us to is, first, derived from good theology. What is God calling us to in this world? What does it mean to be building the kingdom of God? The action is, second, for both individuals and society. We tend to privatize the work of the gospel as only sharing the Good News with individuals for their salvation. The Good News, however, is not only for individuals but also for all of creation, which includes social structures. We are called, therefore, to action on behalf of society as well as individuals. We are called to love God and neighbor with all of our being, and this demands action.

Orthopraxy is acting in appropriate ways to modify our lives. We must see that we are becoming restored to the image of God. This means that we must work on our personal lives in ways that align our behaviors with God's call on us. Dykstra writes, "Faith means turning from an old way to a new way of life."[7] Orthodoxy alone is insufficient. Orthopraxy is also required. "Very truly," said Jesus, "the one who believes in me will also do the works that I do" (John 14:12).

Faith as Orthopathy

Faith is also orthopathy. *Orthopathy* means right passions. We must desire what God desires. This implies that our emotional lives must be transformed and formed. It is important not only that we believe correctly and act correctly but also that we act and believe correctly for the right motives—orthopathy.

What are the qualities of faith as orthopathy? First, faith is trust and confidence. It is our willingness to place our life stories within the story of God and trust God. Trust implies reliance on the sameness and continuity of God. Trust is something that develops; it does not simply exist without prior experience that shapes it, makes it real, and deepens it. We must take the risky step of trusting God, and from there our ability to trust develops as we experience the continuity of God. As Parks puts it, "Faithing is the impulse or force toward, and the putting one's heart upon, that which one trusts as true. . . ."[8] To further an understanding of faith as trust V. Bailey Gillespie writes, "The core of biblical, and more specifically Christian faith, is a trusting kind of self-surrender to the God who reveals

7. Dykstra, "What Is Faith?", p. 58.
8. Parks, *The Critical Years*, p. 21.

himself to the world."[9] The idea of self-surrender is central to orthopathy. Self-surrender is exhibited in our actions but arises first out of our passion for God and the things of God.

Faithfulness is also a quality of orthopathy. We are called to stick with it even though sometimes the reality we experience does not match up to our faith. Faithfulness rests on will or volition. By volition we muster the emotional fortitude to motivate action guided by our belief in God. In some ways orthopathy integrates orthodoxy and orthopraxy. It is the element of faith that brings together understanding and action. Faith is correct belief, correct action, and correct passion.

Maturity: The Vision of Christian Formation

The approach to Christian formation used here is teleological: it is directed toward a vision of what it means to participate in the full stature of Christ. To what end are we directed? What will a maturing Christian person be like? As Alasdair MacIntyre writes, "Without some at least partly determinate conception of the final *telos* there could not be any beginning to a quest."[10] This is what we are attempting to describe with the notion of maturity.

Maturity is one of those words that we shy away from. Our culture assumes that we have no right to discuss what a mature adult should be like, since we are all independent and have a right to be whatever we wish. This uncritical relativism refuses to acknowledge that there are some qualities that a fully functioning adult should exhibit. Within the Christian community, we justify relativism on the grounds that we should not judge others, or we assume that maturity is a behavioristic and static concept that we impose on people. It is clear why we have not wanted to use the idea of maturity, but people who are serious about Christian formation cannot avoid it.

Holiness and Wholeness

The definition of maturity set forth below integrates the theological and psychological issues related to maturity. This becomes diffi-

9. V. Bailey Gillespie, *The Experience of Faith* (Birmingham, Ala.: Religious Education Press, 1988), p. 28.

10. Alasdair MacIntyre, *After Virtue* (Notre Dame, Ind.: University of Notre Dame Press, 1981), pp. 203–4.

cult in light of two basic questions: Can a non-Christian be mature? Can a Christian who is emotionally unstable be mature? The issue may be stated as the idea of holy wholeness. *Holiness* is the term often applied to an explicitly religious definition of maturity. *Wholeness* is a term associated with psychological maturity. Must one be holy to be whole? Must one be whole to be holy?

Often these two notions are either totally isolated from one another or collapsed into each other. Some argue that psychological wholeness has nothing to do with religion and in fact religion may get in the way of wholeness. No doubt religion often does block wholeness. But such religion is not true Christian faith. Some argue that holiness has nothing to do with wholeness and, in fact, it is more important to be holy than whole. Again, this is not an expression of true Christian faith. Some may argue that holiness and wholeness are the same, so that *sanctification* and *self-actualization* are actually synonyms. This is also unacceptable because self-actualization is a fundamentally secular concept that has no vision of the mature human restored to the image of God.

We must bring the concepts of holiness and wholeness together and attempt to describe what Robert Fuller calls "optimal human development."[11] We can assert that "Christian maturity generally correlates with human maturity."[12] We are created in the image of God, and our psychological selves are a part of that image. Optimal human development is the correlation of holiness and wholeness. Non-Christians can experience what may be called psychological wholeness. This is a part of the image of God that remains. Christians can also express holiness without being whole, but, like the whole but unholy non-Christian, the holy but unwhole Christian would not have achieved optimal human development. It is also important to note that a Christian who is psychologically mature is not necessarily mature in faith. Self-actualization is not sanctification. People can neglect the demands of discipleship and remain less than mature in the call of the gospel.

The difficulty in integrating psychology and Christian faith to define maturity is clear. We will now consider five categories that describe optimal human development or the vision of maturing Christian formation: self-objectification, self-criticism, self-transcendence, self-in-community, and self-in-process.

11. Robert C. Fuller, *Religion and the Life Cycle* (Philadelphia: Fortress, 1988).
12. Francis J. Buckley & Donald B. Sharp, *Deepening Christian Life* (New York: Harper & Row, 1987), p. 4.

Self-Objectification

A primary characteristic of mature Christians is their ability to see themselves as objects. This does not mean that they treat themselves with no respect but that they are able to take a third-person perspective on their own lives. Gordon Allport writes that to be self-objectifying means "to be reflective and insightful about one's own life."[13] To be immature means to remain unreflective and without a perspective from which to judge our actions and attitudes.

One of the primary ways of achieving self-objectivity is to strive for integration of all aspects of our lives. Self-objectifying persons are integrated persons. We strive for integration by developing a philosophy of life that brings together the entirety of our lives. We have a summary of what drives us, motivates us, and brings our lives together into a coherent story. For Christians, the gospel is the central story that unifies our lives. We find ourselves as we place ourselves in the story of God in Christ. For Paul that meant being "in Christ," which implies striving toward a full participation in the work of the gospel. The unifying philosophy of Paul's life was his desire to know the fullness of Christ, which meant full participation in the suffering and resurrection of Christ.

This integration of self around the gospel brings with it several characteristics of what Allport calls the "mature religious sentiment." It brings "comprehensiveness" to persons. This means that their faith permeates and unites all aspects of their lives. Integration around the gospel runs not only broad but also deep. That is, we can not only look at their lives from a distance and see faith but also examine them up close and find Christian faith shot through even the most mundane and hidden aspects of their lives. This integratedness around a philosophy of life also brings moral direction. It is the basis of moral decision making.

Self-objectifying persons are also responsible selves. They recognize that they are ultimately accountable to God for their lives. Yes, we are formed in part by our environments, but we must take the responsibility to attempt to move beyond the problems that these may create for us. The gospel gives hope to those who have experienced oppressive environments. This implies that we are to become more autonomous, that is, to be less susceptible to the environment and more in control of our own lives. It means that we interact with that environment and can decide what is proper and what is not.

13. Gordon Allport, *The Individual and His Religion* (New York: Macmillan, 1950), p. 60.

This does not imply some heroic sort of independence, because we are called not to be independent but interdependent. It implies that we take responsibility for our own lives and faith. As such, our faith then becomes our own, not someone else's. It is no longer the result of what our parents taught us, although it may incorporate much of their faith. It is what Allport calls a well-differentiated faith. We have become responsible persons, have sorted through the issues, and have affirmed a faith and a life that are our own.

Being responsible selves also implies that we are self-disciplined—that we are not dependent on others for motivation to complete our tasks but are motivated from within. Self-disciplined persons are in control of daily routines and find time to care for all aspects of their lives. They allocate time to nurture their souls, to fulfill their obligations, and to care for others.

Self-objectifying persons are also stable. Stability does not imply that they are unmovable or unchangeable. It implies that they can assess the events of their lives in the light of the unifying story of their lives. This allows them to discern which changes are appropriate and which are not. Stability means that they can withstand the assault of personal, interpersonal, and social problems and remain integrated persons.

Self-Criticism

Self-criticism is the ability to be observers of our own lives. We can step outside the flow of our lives, look up and down the river, and discern a pattern. Self-assessment is necessary. In Romans 12:3 Paul exhorts every believer, "Think with sober judgment." In the context, Paul is writing about discerning what gifts we have to offer the body of Christ. But we can extend the advice to include the wisdom of taking an honest look at who we are and what we have to offer out of the totality of our lives.

A corresponding issue here is the self-deceptive nature of human beings. We easily fool ourselves into believing that we are more important than we are. We begin to believe our own press. This is particularly true of those who achieve acclaim and position. As Stanley Hauerwas writes, "The greater the integrity of our character, the more we are liable to self-deception and fault."[14] We suffer the con-

---

14. Stanley Hauerwas, "Character, Narrative, and Growth in the Christian Life," in *Toward Moral and Religious Maturity*, ed. James W. Fowler and Antoine Vergote (Morristown, N.J.: Silver Burdett, 1980), p. 451.

sequences of a tarnished human nature, and self-criticism is one way to overcome this.

To be self-critical also implies that we recognize the complexity of life. There are no easy answers, no matter how much we wish there were. It is clear from observing how church and society respond to the easy-answer gurus that we all crave easy answers. But the Christian faith is complex, and everyday living further complicates the issues. Self-critical persons recognize this and work out a faith that is critically appropriated and not simplistically bought.

Recognizing the complexity of life also means learning to live with its ambiguity. It means recognizing that our knowledge is approximate and tentative. "For now we see in a mirror, dimly, but then we will see face to face. Now I know only in part; then I will know fully, even as I have been fully known" (1 Cor. 13:12). Paul acknowledges what is sometimes painful: that we cannot know fully. This leads us to tolerate the ambiguities of life and to be humble about our knowledge or views of Christian faith.

The realization of ambiguity leads us to be flexible about our own positions and the positions of others. This can help us to avoid what Erik Erikson calls "pseudospeciation." By this he means the attitude that "mykind is humankind." Everyone must believe and behave like me. Pseudospeciation engenders a spiritual imperialism that forces our views on others. Mature individuals are flexible. They hold firmly to personal beliefs but are open to change and to others' opinions. This is not to suggest that maturity is mere relativism. Christian maturity holds fast to essentials of the Christian faith while tolerating diversity in non-essentials. It also calls for critical reflection on other positions; therefore, it is not a posture that affirms nonsensical or unthoughtful positions. Mature Christians take to heart both elements of Paul's instruction, "but test everything; hold fast to what is good" (1 Thess. 5:21).

Self-critical persons are aware of the complexity of life, appreciate symbol, live with ambiguity, and are flexible. Each of these qualities tends to be found in persons who have a healthy sense of humor. Allport states, "Another road favorable to integration is humor, man's principal technique for getting rid of irrelevancies."[15] Humor is an arena for self-criticism. Maturing persons are playful in all areas of life, faith included. They can poke fun at themselves and their theology and not be consumed by an egocentric over-seriousness. Matur-

15. Allport, *The Individual and His Religion*, p. 104.

ing persons who are characterized by self-criticism exhibit a type of faith that is truly a journey or quest. Daniel Batson and Larry Ventis describe religion as quest as a religion that has the characteristics of complexity, doubt, and tentativeness.[16]

Self-Transcendence

The primary distinction between optimal human development, which is grounded in Christian theology, and a non-Christian notion of human development is the end or purpose of development. Typically, a non-Christian view of human development locates the end of development in the individual. A Christian view, however, asserts that the end of human development rests beyond self-actualization in our companionship with God.

James Fowler asserts that our most serious modern heresy may be the idea that our end is self-actualization or the belief that we are "self-grounded" persons.[17] We are not self-grounded and should not be, yet this does not imply self-annihilation. Walter Conn writes, "As an image suggestive of the authentic dynamism of the Christian spiritual life, self-transcendence stands in total opposition to the image of self-sacrifice understood as a denial, renunciation, abnegation, repudiation, sacrifice, or other negation of the true self. . . . The self is not negated through transcendence; rather, it is realized in its authentic being. Self-transcendence is authentic self-realization."[18]

Likewise, we must reject the current self-esteem cult that places self-actualization as the end of human development. While we must not deny the importance of the self, we are called to give the self away. Nonetheless, this implies that there is a self to give.

Some psychological theorists recognize the notion of self-transcendence and interpret human development in its light. Here we are interested in concepts of healthy human development as self-transcending in nature. We are not to be concerned with our development simply for its own sake. We are called to develop beyond ourselves to God. As the Westminster Shorter Catechism so aptly states, "Man's chief end is to glorify God, and to enjoy him forever." We

16. C. Daniel Batson and Larry Ventis, *The Religious Experience: A Social-Psychological Perspective* (New York: Oxford University Press, 1982), p. 149.

17. James W. Fowler, *Becoming Adult, Becoming Christian* (New York: Harper & Row, 1984), p. 101.

18. Walter Conn, *Christian Conversion: A Developmental Interpretation of Autonomy and Surrender* (Mahwah, N.J.: Paulist, 1986), p. 22.

turn now to consider both theological and psychological dimensions of self-transcendence.

Reinhold Niebuhr wrote that man "cannot find himself without finding a center beyond himself."[19] Jesus said, "My food is to do the will of him who sent me and to complete his work" (John 4:34). In other passages Jesus indicated that what gave him meaning was to do the will of the Father. He also said that only those who do the will of the Father will see the kingdom of God (Matt. 7:21). Clearly, the gospel calls us beyond fulfilling our own wills and desires to fulfilling God's. If we are to become fully human, we will seek to do the will of God, to transcend ourselves.

If we ask what it is to do God's will, the answer is, "You shall love the Lord your God with all your heart, and with all your soul, and with all your strength, and with all your mind; and your neighbor as yourself" (Luke 10:27). In loving God we escape the heresy of self-actualization, and the parable of the good Samaritan shows that it is in loving our neighbors that we show our love for God (Luke 10:30–37; cf. 1 John 4:20).

Paul's affirmation of self-transcendence is summed up in Philippians 1:21: "For to me, living is Christ and dying is gain." Here we discover that the fulfillment of human development culminates in our death, which places us in the presence of God. Paul clearly has in mind something other than self-actualization as the goal of human development. This is also affirmed in Philippians 2:5–11, which exhorts us to have the mind of Christ, who emptied himself to serve others. To be maturing Christians we must become self-transcendent.

This leads to two important aspects of self-transcendence; allocentrism and generativity. Allocentrism is other-centeredness. It is the ability to care for others. Hospitality is one way to describe this quality of maturity. Again we appeal to the parable of the good Samaritan. Not only the Samaritan shows hospitality, but also the innkeeper. He willingly keeps the injured man at his inn while he recovers; although he is paid, this still implies his willingness to care for the man. He is willing to take in the stranger, to create a place for recovery. Henri Nouwen states that hospitality is "a fundamental attitude toward our fellow human being. . . ."[20] Hospitable persons

19. Reinhold Niebuhr, quoted in Ernest L. Boyer, *College: The Undergraduate Experience in America* (New York: Harper & Row, 1987), p. 279.

20. Henri Nouwen, *Reaching Out: The Three Movements of Spiritual Life* (New York: Doubleday, 1975), p. 48.

make room for the stranger or friend. They create a free and friendly space.

Part of hospitality is reconciliation. Reconciliation is the making right of relationships and situations. In 2 Corinthians 5 we are called to be reconcilers—to share the ministry of reconciliation. Allocentric persons exemplify hospitality and reconciliation.

Generativity is defined by Erikson as the ability to care for the upcoming generation. It implies procreativity, productivity, and creativity. It can express itself in generating human life and products to serve society and in the creative acts of human beings that give vision, hope, and care to the upcoming generation. Erikson defines care as "a widening commitment to take care of the persons, the products, and the ideas one has learned to care for."[21] Self-transcending persons care for and generate life for the coming generation. More will be said about this later, but I mention it here as central to self-transcendence.

In summary, self-transcending persons are other-centered, being agents of hospitality and reconciliation. They are also generative, caring for others and showing preference for them.

Self-in-Community

Daniel Jenkins asserts that two aspects are vital to Christian maturity. "The first is that this maturity is known only in relationship, . . . [the] second, [that] we have a mutual interest in each other's growth toward maturity."[22] Maturing Christians recognize the necessity of community. As Sharon Parks states, "The pilgrimage of faith must be made in the company of others."[23] This is to be a community of mutuality and reciprocity; as the community contributes to our growth, we contribute to its growth and the growth of its members.

Being created in the image of the triune God implies that we are created to be in interdependent relationships. By gathering follow-

21. Erik H. Erikson, *The Life Cycle Completed: A Review* (New York: Norton, 1982), p. 67.

22. Daniel Jenkins, *Christian Maturity* and *Christian Success* (Philadelphia: Fortress, 1982), p. 4.

23. Sharon Parks, "Love Tenderly," in Sharon Parks, Walter Brueggemann, and Thomas Groome, *To Act Justly, Love Tenderly, Walk Humbly* (Mahwah, N.J.: Paulist, 1986), p. 33.

ers around him, Jesus implicitly affirmed that participating in community plays a central role in maturing. Paul speaks more specifically about the role of faith community in his letters. Particularly in 1 Corinthians 12–14 and Ephesians 4, he asserts the importance of the whole body of Christ in building up the community of faith. The community is a place for us to grow together in truth and love. In it are identified the gifts each of us brings to the community for the purpose of building one another up. The community of faith also functions as a place where our lives are shared. We are called to rejoice with those who rejoice and to mourn with those who mourn. The faith community provides a context for growth in maturity.

Consider the psychological importance of community and relationships. "The human being does not compose meaning all alone," writes Parks. "The individual person is not the sole actor in the drama of human development."[24] Erikson's interactionist approach affirms the importance of the ethos, or social setting, in which we develop. This ethos brings to us ways of being and thinking that deeply affect our developmental trajectories. Erikson also points out that the historical moment influences human development. In other words, not only the ethos but also the particular point in history in which we live make a difference. Being an eighteen-year-old in 1989 is different from being an eighteen-year-old in either 1940 or 1964.

More specifically, consider how communities function to assist our development. Building on Robert Kegan's work, Laurent Daloz describes the functions of a community. "Environments," he tells us, "do three things; they provide confirmation, contradiction, and continuity."[25] By being a community of confirmation, a faith community offers persons a place to develop their identities and to discover what they have to offer in the service of the kingdom of God. When persons begin to form an identity, the community is there to confirm and affirm when the developing identity is congruent with the values of the community. Kegan describes this role as that of a "holding environment" where persons have space to explore alternative Christian identities. The community also functions to confirm the gifts and talents of its members. Theologically and psychologically, it is important that each person discover something she can do

24. Parks, *The Critical Years*, p. 61.
25. Laurent Daloz, *Effective Teaching and Mentoring: Realizing the Transformational Power of Adult Learning Experiences* (San Francisco: Jossey-Bass, 1986), p. 192.

and is competent at doing. The community can be a place to discover, test, and develop these gifts. It is also important to reaffirm a theology of giftedness that sees gifts as primarily not for individuals but for the development of the community. Gifts are to be used in mission. The community provides a context for mission, a place to find where we will be of service to the community, to society, and to the kingdom of God.

The confirming role of the community is fine as long as our identities are developing in acceptable ways and we are using our gifts appropriately. But this often does not happen, and the ways in which we make sense out of our lives often conflict with the community. We might need to find a new community, but it may just as well be that the community is providing the conflict necessary for us to develop in more appropriate ways. This is the function of contradiction. A community must not only support but also challenge. It must provide for its members the opportunities to be confronted with the reality of their direction, which may be counterproductive to their maturing. This implies, however, that the community is self-critical enough to be cautious and recognize its own shortcomings. The community is an agent of dissonance that causes persons to rethink the direction of their identities.

One of the important conditions for us when forming identities is to have a community that not only confirms and contradicts but also provides continuity. By providing continuity, the community develops a story and a character that give it the right both to confirm and to contradict. If we are a part of a community with no history, we hesitate to allow it to play a significant role in our development. But by providing continuity the community provides a story into which we can fold our stories so that we have a sense of stability. Dykstra writes, "The character of the community shapes the character of its people."[26] This stability is important when we are being challenged by alternative stories of life that are less than acceptable for the maturing Christian.

In summary, maturing Christians are part of a community in which they can develop their identities, explore their gifts, and discover ways of being in mission. The community offers them a place of support and challenge as they traverse the path of Christian maturing.

26. Craig Dykstra, *Vision and Character: A Christian Educator's Alternative to Kohlberg* (Mahwah, N.J.: Paulist, 1981), p. 55.

Self-in-Process

We have already established in our discussions of both the theological and the psychological nature of persons that we are beings in the process of development. We now assert that a processive outlook on life is a quality of maturing persons. Our culture emphasizes stability and unchangeability. If we were mature we would not change: we would be in the same place, with the same job, with the same haircut, and with the same attitudes as long as we lived. No doubt part of this desire for continuity is good and reflects actual human experience. There are aspects of human character that we hope will continue across the life span. But to deny the same reality to process and change is to run from the inevitable. Our lives are more of a video tape or narrative than a snapshot. How sad it would be if our children never developed beyond the age of eight or nine!

This is also the case with what we have called optimal human development or Christian human development. "Fundamental to the Christian view of man is, therefore, an insistence on a process of growth,"[27] wrote Bouwsma. Conversely, "the Christian conception of immaturity is the refusal to grow, the inability to cope with an open and indeterminate future (that is, the future itself), in effect the rejection of life as a process."[28] Allport asserts that mature religion is heuristic or tentative. Life is a process; in particular, Christian life is a process. Therefore, we do not speak of maturity but of maturing.

These are the five categories around which we can describe maturing Christian persons. Maturing Christians are self-objectifying; they have established at the center of their lives the gospel, which focuses them and allows them to live responsibly. They are self-critical; they do not merely accept a simplistic gospel in the face of complex realities. They understand that life is ambiguous, and therefore they hold loosely to their dimly perceived meanings. They are self-transcending; they recognize that the end or purpose of human development is not the self but the self in service of God's kingdom. They are on a trajectory away from self-centeredness toward God-centeredness. Maturing Christians recognize that they are created to be in relationship; the faith community provides them a context in which to mature and serve. Finally, maturing Christians see themselves as in process. A friend is fond of saying, "The journey is the destination."

27. William Bouwsma, "Christian Adulthood," in *Adulthood*, ed. Erik H. Erikson (New York: Norton, 1978), p. 87.

28. Ibid., p. 87.

9

Principles of Christian Formation

Three key principles describe the process of Christian formation. We will look first at the developmental principle as it relates to Christian maturing, second at conversion and nurture, and third at the interactive nature of Christian formation.

Christian Formation Is Developmental

The primary principle of Christian formation is that it is developmental. It moves from simple or less complex forms to more complex forms. This is not to depict Christian formation in a structural-cognitive developmental way. Christian formation does not occur in discrete, invariant, hierarchical, sequential stages. Rather than necessarily progressive, the movement of Christian formation is processional. Regression and fixation are possible. Christians may forget their first love.

Calling Christian formation developmental implies that it is in process and is dynamic. It also implies that it is intimately connected with the processes of human development. It could be said that human development is a necessary but not a sufficient cause for Christian formation.

Christian formation as developmental embraces both change and constancy. Sometimes advocates of a developmental approach overlook the constants in life. Some things remain relatively constant over the course of the life cycle, and we need to appreciate them.

But a developmental approach reminds us that Christian formation is not static and unchanging. It is changing, and many times this frightens us. Consider, for instance, the first time an adolescent questions faith. The reaction of the parent or adult is to squelch the question in hopes of "saving" the faith of the adolescent. We know, however, that the questions will come, that life is changing, and that attempting to squelch the growth of Christian faith is as detrimental as attempting to retard the physical growth of our children.

Christian formation also includes critical periods, or what Robert Havighurst calls "teachable moments." These are moments when a person is ready to learn or understand a concept. There are times when, because of general patterns of growth and individual circumstances, people are not ready to deal with certain issues. This is the case for faith as well. Children in the concrete thinking stage are not ready to deal with the biblical text in its theological and literary complexity. They are, however, ready to appreciate the story of God's salvation as told in Scripture. There are also individual patterns of growth. One child may begin to read at three, another at five or six. Developmental schemes can only describe parameters, not norms. Christian faith is similar in that people's life courses may take them in certain directions that affect growth in faith. Traumatic experiences are the most obvious example of this. The loss of a loved one or unexpected grief or joy may precipitate growth in faith. Christian faith, therefore, is influenced by both general and individual teachable moments.

Understanding Christian formation as developmental makes us both comfortable and uncomfortable. It allows us to relax when we realize that we are on a lifelong journey and have a long way to go. It also creates increased self-responsibility as we realize that we are called to an ever-growing faith. The maturing that we exhibited yesterday is not sufficient for today. This implies that even though we may have experienced detrimental situations, we are ultimately responsible for our own Christian formation.

Christian Formation Includes Both Conversion and Nurture

When a developmental approach to Christian formation is advocated, one of the first questions to arise is the place of conversion. Some argue that a developmental approach has no place for conversion, which makes it unacceptable in their understanding of Christian formation. Others simply want to know where conversion fits in a scheme that is predominantly nurture oriented. We will address this issue by defining conversion and then discussing its relationship to nurture and formation.

Consider the following exchanges about conversion.

1. "Have you been converted? If so, tell me about it."
   Response: "Yes, I have been converted; which conversion do you want to know about?"
2. "Have you been converted?"
   Response: "I'm not sure. I am a Christian, I'm sure of that, but I'm not sure what you mean by conversion."
3. "Have you been converted?"
   Response: "Yes!!!! On May 3, 1983, at 5:00 P.M., in a restaurant with Joe. I was having a hamburger; he had a salad."
4. "Have you been converted?"
   Response: "Yes, but it was not very exciting. I just sort of realized my need for Christ and quietly, to myself, said yes to God."

Each of these—and more could be explored—represents a different way in which conversion can legitimately be understood and experienced. Our problem is that we have tended to straitjacket the conversion experience in the language and mode that was common during the revivals in America. What we need is a more balanced definition of conversion that allows for the varieties of experiences of God's grace. At root in each of these scenarios is the reorientation of the person. The Greek word *metanoia* implies a turning around or redirecting of our lives. "Through religious conversion's experience, an all-embracing goal is obtained and focused, around which the experiences of life will be grounded and interpreted,"[1] writes V. Bailey Gillespie. This reorientation can be of greater or lesser degrees of change. "For some," writes Walter Conn, "the change may be only one of degree, a question of further growth or development. But, for others, the required change will be much more fundamental."[2] This takes away some of the extremist language

1. V. Bailey Gillespie, *Religious Conversion and Personal Identity* (Birmingham, Ala.: Religious Education Press, 1979), p. 171.
2. Walter Conn, *Christian Conversion: A Developmental Interpretation of Autonomy and Surrender* (Mahwah, N.J.: Paulist, 1986), p. 17.

about conversion that requires everyone to have a radical conversion in which he gives up the horrors of the past (but of course he remembers the past enough to tell us the sordid details we love to hear!). There are also degrees of emotion involved. For some conversion is highly emotional; for others it is a calm, objective experience.

Whatever the degree of change or emotion, a Christian conversion is required of us all and will include a change of the total self. It is a reorientation that includes orthodoxy, orthopraxy, and orthopathy—reorientation to right belief, right practice, and right passion.

This reorientation is described by Jesus in John 3 as a new birth. The metaphor has been used (overused) to describe the joy of coming to know the true purpose of life. The problem with this view is that it ignores the pain of birth. There is joy, no doubt, but birth is a painful, messy, and life-threatening experience. "Tradition," writes Leroy Howe, "has not typically spoken of the conversion dynamic as itself necessarily accompanied by the pain of physical and psychic disarray."[3] Conversion must involve painful reinterpretation of one's past, facing up to one's sin and failure, and dealing with the ongoing task of working out one's salvation with fear and trembling. It must be seen as a sickness unto health. I remember a patient in the hospital who was in great pain but needed physical therapy to alleviate it. As the nurse massaged the patient, his response was, "Nurse, it hurts so good!" We must correct our overly joyous approach to conversion and recognize the pain of new birth and say, "It hurts so good!"

We must also recognize that there is Conversion and there are conversions. There is a point when people must, as Frederick Buechner says, "come to their senses," but there are also continuing moments of conversion when we turn further toward God. We are not converted, we are being converted. The initial conversion is just the beginning of a series of conversions that leads us further to the call of Christian maturing.

This immediately raises the issue of the relationship of conversion to nurture, of transformation to formation. For some, advocating a developmental approach means denying the necessity of conversion. For others, emphasizing conversion means denying the ongoing trajectory of Christian maturing and creating a static view of Christian

3. Leroy Howe, "A Developmental Perspective on Conversion," *Perkins Journal* 33 (Fall 1979), p. 35.

formation. The problem is that an either/or situation has been created. This is not true to reality. Conversion and nurture function together; formation and transformation are an ongoing process. On the one hand, formation can operate as a "catalyst for conversion."[4] As we come under the influence of the teachings of the Christian faith, those teachings can raise questions about our relationship with God, leading in turn to conversion. Nurture or formation can create meaningful frustration, enabling us to see our need for transformation. On the other hand, once we are transformed we are indeed new persons and in need of nurturing in our new lives. We need a new language and a new way of understanding our past, present, and future. Clearly, there is an interplay between conversion and nurture. Conn states that transformation depends on formation, adding that if formation is good, "it may, just because it is good, prevent the person from being aware of the need for repentance and decision."[5] We must take care to realize that the gospel calls us to repentance. We must also realize that the ways people come to Christian faith are many. Nurture can and must lead persons to recognize their need for conversion. We must also remember that conversion creates a whole new situation that demands ongoing nurture and formation.

Christian Formation Is Interactive

When we consider what affects Christian formation, our answer must take into account the complex web of human life. It is an interactive process that includes the person himself or herself, the family, the culture of origin, the historical moment in which one is living, and the involvement of the Holy Spirit in the person's life. Christian formation must be understood as including each of these elements, but it must also be understood as greater than the sum of its parts. A mysterious interaction of all of these elements influences Christian growth. Also, Christian formation takes place in real human experience. We sometimes isolate Christian faith from everyday experiences and obligations, making it irrelevant to real life. But Christian formation *is* real life. If we wall off our Christian formation from real life, we only pretend.

4. See Mary Boys, "Conversion as a Foundation of Religious Education," *Religious Education 77* (March–April 1982): 211–25.

5. Conn, *Christian Conversion,* p. 207.

The Individual

The acts and intentionss of persons contribute to their Christian formation. This may seem too obvious even to discuss, but in our day it seems that everyone and everything other than individuals are either credited or blamed for the way in which they develop. If we are irresponsible, we are simply a product of our environment. Environmental notions of Christian formation seem to imply that if we place persons in the right environments and inculcate them with the right information they will come out as wonderful Christian products. All of this neglects the reality of the individual person. After all, this is one of the primary contributions of Christian theology to our understanding of persons. We must preserve the person and in so doing acknowledge the significant role we play in our own growth. This includes the self as both a physical and psychological being. Our physical makeup influences our Christian formation. For example, consider the relationship of our bodies to our self-concept and our self-esteem. How we look affects how we think and feel about ourselves. This self-concept in turn affects how we understand our relationship to God. If we feel cheated because we are not as attractive as we want to be, we wonder about God. If, however, we are attractive, this can have either a positive or a negative effect on our faith. We might be humbly grateful, but we also might become so vain that we cannot see God. Or consider handicapped people. How do we encounter pain and illness? Our physical condition affects our growth in faith.

We are also psychological beings. We are whole persons with personalities and aspirations that influence our formation. The individual is a human being facing the psychological crises and tasks of human development, and these are points for growth in faith. Our psychological makeup also affects our Christian formation. We can describe in general ways the temperaments of people and the ways they typically interact with others. These psychological types affect how people grow in faith. Some people are more expressive of emotions than others; as such, they will probably seek out faith communities that are more emotionally expressive. Much of the debate over worship style has been construed wrongly as a theological question when in fact it is simply a result of the varieties of psychological makeup that God gives.

6. Craig Dykstra and Sharon Parks, eds., *Faith Development and Fowler* (Birmingham, Ala.: Religious Education Press, 1986), p. 61.

Emphasis on the individual raises the issue of intentionality. As Craig Dykstra writes, "Intentionality also suggests the idea that who we become is to a major extent our own responsibility."[6] We must take responsibility for the direction of our Christian formation. We do so in a variety of ways, but primarily by practicing the disciplines of the Christian life. When we take responsibility to pray, meditate, study, and read Scripture, we intentionalize our Christian formation. Although we are not the sole creators of our lives, we do participate intentionally with all the factors that create the drama of Christian human development.

The Family

The family is the primary influence on Christian formation in early life. The examples of parents, siblings, and extended family members shape children's faith. In childhood we are more dependent on others for our understanding of ourselves and therefore more dependent on them for our understanding of our Christian selves. Today we are more aware of the negative influence of dysfunctional families than we once were. The effects of abuse are powerful and prolonged. We must acknowledge these problems; at the same time we must be careful not to reduce Christian growth to therapy.

We must also appreciate the effects of what Erik Erikson refers to as the "cogwheeling of generations." By this he means that we are in a cycle of generations of family and friends, each of which affects the others. Grandparents bring to grandchildren something of who they are in ways parents cannot. Children likewise affect parents and grandparents. We must recognize the power of generations in the process of Christian formation.

The Community of Faith

The faith community to which believers commit themselves influences their Christian formation through the broad effect of the community's tradition and the more direct effect of persons closely related to them. Both broad tradition and close acquaintances have tacit and explicit impact on Christian formation. The community's tradition is the Christian heritage from which that particular faith community arises. A multitude of Protestant, Catholic, and Orthodox traditions shape how faith communities understand the faith. A community that traces its heritage to traditions that place primary emphasis on grace in the believer's life will understand Christian formation quite differently from a community that traces its roots to a tradition that emphasizes the responsibility of the believer for growth in faith.

Differences in worship and polity will also influence Christian formation. This influence will be both tacit and explicit. Tacit, or subtle, influences are present but do not draw our overt attention; nevertheless they affect our faith. These are what John Westerhoff refers to as elements of the "hidden curriculum." They are aspects of the faith community's tradition that teach in unintentional ways.

Explicit aspects of the faith community also influence the development of its members. In particular, persons who are responsible for teaching in the community bring their own biases to how Christian faith is understood. They may not recognize the hidden elements of their teaching; nevertheless, they will communicate certain ways of understanding the Christian faith that are directly affected by these elements. Likewise, teachers have some explicit biases that they knowingly share and teach. In these and many other ways the faith community to which one belongs directly affects the course of Christian formation.

Culture

All one needs to do is to visit another country or even another ethnic group in America to realize the differences that culture can bring to an understanding of Christian formation. It is to be hoped that we appreciate what these cultural differences teach us about Christian faith. Society also affects the ways in which we understand Christian formation. In America we feel the effects of a Christian faith that may be too interwoven with how we do politics. In Europe, the church is dealing with the effects of a tradition of state churches. Much more could be said here, but the point is that we must appreciate the roles of culture and society in Christian formation.

Moment in History

Along with each of the above issues, the moment in history in which we find ourselves affects our Christian formation. As I sit and write this, we are celebrating the twentieth anniversary of America's landing on the moon. There is much about 1969 that gave shape to

Christian formation. I think back on my own adolescence and how I was influenced by what was called the "Jesus Movement." This was actually an extension of the counterculture of the day. We are developing as persons in a family, in a particular faith community, and in a particular culture and society, and we are a part of these at a particular point in history that will influence each of these and therefore our Christian formation.

The Holy Spirit

We are not simply natural beings but also beings connected with the supernatural—with our Creator. When we come to Christian faith, the Holy Spirit actively participates in the process of Christian formation. In John's Gospel, we find the Holy Spirit guiding believers to truth. In Philippians, he completes the work begun in each of us. There is much about ourselves and the process of Christian growth that we will ignore or refuse to attempt. There are things about ourselves that must be worked on that are simply too painful for us to attempt. Eustace found this out in *The Voyage of the Dawn Treader*. In this book, which is a part of C. S. Lewis's Chronicles of Narnia, Eustace finds that he is, due to his greed, a dragon. He is rejected by his fellow travelers and is remorseful for his greed. At this point Aslan, the God figure of Narnia, comes to Eustace and calls him to follow him if he wishes to do away with his dragonhood. Eustace follows Aslan to a pool of water, where Aslan leads him to start stripping away the dragon scales. Eustace does so but finds that he remains a dragon. Aslan then explains that he, Aslan, must help. So he digs his claws deep into Eustace's skin. Eustace feels the pain but soon finds he is a new person without the dragon skin. I've done an injustice to the actual story, but the point is clear. The Holy Spirit cooperates with us in Christian formation in ways that may be painful but are necessary. This is not to isolate the Spirit's role to painful moments, for he is involved in all of our growth. It is simply to illustrate how the Spirit may operate.

The last two chapters presented broad issues of an approach to Christian formation that integrates theology and psychology. The approach is developmental in nature. The preceding chapter began by addressing a definition of faith that is both theologically and psychologically useful. It then described the vision of Christian formation. This allows us to see clearly the trajectory of Christian formation. Finally, this chapter addressed general principles of a developmental approach to Christian formation. These included an explanation of what *developmental* means in relation to Christian formation, how conversion is understood, and what components influence the interactive nature of Christian formation. We turn now to the cycles of Christian formation.

Part 4

Cycles of
Christian Formation

10

Cycles of Christian Formation in Childhood

With the basic aspects of our approach to Christian formation outlined, we move now to a description of cycles of Christian formation across the lifespan. The cycles here described are clearly derived from an Eriksonian approach to human development. They may, however, differ from the approximate age periods some have placed with Erik Erikson's stages. They are my attempt to depict the trajectory of optimal human development in a predominantly psychosocial fashion. I use Erikson's theoretical scheme, but I assign names to the cycles primarily to describe the tasks of Christian formation common to them.

The image that works best to visualize the cycles is that of a spiral. Images of a ladder or stair steps are misleading. Both connote too much prescription and achievement as one "qualifies" to move to the next rung or step. The spiral begins at the base with small circles that move upward and outward, encompassing more and more within their boundaries. This image conveys a sense of direction: the individual is going somewhere. The cycles describe the Christian journey or quest. The spiral also conveys that as the circles expand, so does the individual's self-responsibility. Believers become increasingly responsible for their own quests as those who have had early responsibility must relinquish their control over the process.

Our discussion of each cycle includes a description of the basic crisis and task, the emergent virtue, the ritualization, and the form of thinking associated with it. There are seven cycles of Christian formation—not eight, as in Erikson's theory. The difference consists of combining Erikson's second and third cycles into one cycle of Christian formation. This reflects the opinion that the issues of Christian formation for these age periods are quite similar.

All of the aspects mentioned above, except the form of thinking, are found in Erikson's descriptions of the psychosocial life cycle. They will be presented as polarities, as in Erikson's theory. As Eugene Wright states, "Erikson is consistently dialectical in his thinking."[1] There are counter-forces working against the healthy development of the person. Some level of the negative side of each polarity is necessary to protect the individual from being harmed by a society that is less than caring. Erikson typically speaks of a "favorable ratio" in the resolution of each cycle. This means that the positive pole of the cycle should outweigh the negative, but there must be some level of the negative for a realistic view of life. The cycles of Christian formation also partake of such polarities. The polarities are the tensions implicit throughout the life cycle in the struggle toward a maturing Christian faith.

Definition of Nomenclature

Crisis

A definition of the aspects presented in each cycle is in order. Each cycle is described primarily by the crisis of that period. As Erikson states, "Crisis at any age does not necessarily connote a threat of catastrophe but rather a turning point, a crucial period of increased vulnerability and heightened potential."[2]

The word *crisis* can imply a more negative idea than is meant. *Crisis* means a point in which particular issues must be dealt with. A crisis is similar to a teachable moment. It is a time when the individual and the environment dictate that particular issues need attention. This does not imply that the crisis is only present during that particular age. Each of the cycles is present in some form prior to its time of ascendency and will continue to be worked with after its particular time. But each crisis has a point in which it is at the forefront of the tasks of Christian formation and after which it will continue to be

1. J. Eugene Wright, Jr., *Erikson: Identity and Religion* (New York: Harper & Row, 1982), p. 41.
2. Erik H. Erikson, "Reflections on Dr. Borg's Life Cycle," in Erikson, ed., *Adulthood* (New York: Norton, 1978), p. 5.

part of the work of Christian formation. Thus, nurturing faith is a crisis of infancy and early childhood; however, it will continue to be an important aspect of Christian formation after that age. No one ever outgrows the need for a nurturing environment. It must be said, however, that a negative resolution of each crisis at its point of ascendency will result in difficulty in the resolution of subsequent crises.

Virtue

The word *virtue* implies a quality of character that becomes a part of the developing Christian's sense of self. By *virtue* Erikson meant strength, vitality, and courage.[3] Christian faith adds to this the idea of soulfulness, a quality of character that motivates and points the person in the proper direction. It is probably in the virtues that the integration of psychology and theology is most clearly found. Like crises, virtues have their opposites. Erikson calls these antipathies. They are the weaknesses of character or the lack of courage that come about from a negative resolution of particular crises. They become obstacles to further growth in Christian faith; therefore, we may call them vices.

Ritualizations

Ritualizations are ways in which persons interact at particular times. They guide how people relate to each other and to the institutions of which they are parts. Opposite to ritualizations are ritualisms, compulsive forms of relating that are performed in meaningless and repetitive ways. Ritualisms are habitual behaviors that restrict human relationships rather than freeing them.

An example may be helpful. My son and I have a particular way of dealing with bedtime. The ritualization includes a back ride to bed, a glass of water, a back rub, and my son's hiding under his covers and my corresponding inability to find him. As I stand by his bed and lament his disappearance, he bursts from under the covers to surprise me. After this he can sleep. My daughter has also found this ritualized act important. Doing this night after night assures them of the security of our relationships and calms their nighttime fears. It is a form of interrelating that delivers the message that all is well. It may become a ritualism if it gets so compulsive that it interferes

3. See Erik H. Erikson, *Insight and Responsibility* (New York: Norton, 1964), p. 19.

with a sense of well-being. These forms of interrelating also affect Christian formation. How we relate can help or hurt ongoing Christian formation.

Cognition

Finally, cognition is how persons make sense out of their environment at particular times. Piaget's theory of cognitive development gives shape to this aspect of each cycle.

Cycles

These cycles are not given to judge the quality of a person's Christian formation but to describe the direction of optimal human development, thereby identifying appropriate ways of educating for Christian formation in each cycle. The cycles are as follows:

Infancy: Nurturing versus Neglecting
Childhood: Enculturating and Training versus Ignoring
Early Adolescence: Belonging versus Alienating
Adolescence: Searching versus Entrenching
Young Adulthood: Consolidating versus Fragmenting
Middle Adulthood: Re-appraising versus Re-entrenching
Later Adulthood: Anticipating versus Dreading

Christian Formation in Childhood

Infancy: Nurturing versus Neglecting

We often forget to consider infancy as a time of Christian formation. We think that, because infants lack language and reading skills, they cannot be about the process of forming faith. This unfortunate view relegates Christian formation to a matter of mere intellect.

It is important in this phase of life that the infant senses the nurturing of self and faith. Nurturing implies that we care for and give to the infant. Infants develop pre-images of God as they see parents who are the givers of care, both physical and emotional.[4] James Fowler refers to this as a period of undifferentiated faith in which

4. See Ana-Maria Rizzuto, *The Birth of the Living God: A Psychoanalytic Study* (Chicago: University of Chicago Press, 1979).

infants do not have a developed sense of self or faith. Theirs will be, from now until at least adolescence, a borrowed faith. They will know the love of God by being loved by those who love God.

As is clear already, the significant others who nurture the faith of infants are usually the parents. It is their responsibility. The danger here is that, for a variety of reasons, faith may be neglected. Parents may not realize the importance of the developing image of God that is shaped at this time. They may think themselves too busy to take time to attend to nurturing the infant. The way to foster faith in this stage is to care for the child in the name of Christ.

The psychosocial crisis of this cycle is trust versus mistrust. Here Erikson finds the basis for the healthy personality. Here, also, is the foundation for a healthy life of faith in Christ. Trust, according to Erikson, is reliance on the sameness and continuity of those who provide for the infant. Without trust we cannot develop meaningful relationships. Yet trust must not be naive gullibility. There must be a favorable ratio, a polarity of trust and mistrust. We must, in order to survive in an untrustworthy world, have some mistrust. If not, we will be manipulated and hurt. This is true in Christian formation as well. The call to *blind* trust or faith often can be a call to follow someone or some movement that seeks only its own good and is untrustworthy.

Erikson also points out that it is the parents' faith that seems to be a cornerstone for developing a sense of trust in the infant. It is from parents' faith that infants must derive a healthy sense of dependence on God that nurtures a sense of trust.

The danger is that an unfavorable ratio of trust to mistrust will develop. This implies that an infant finds her caretakers untrustworthy and neglectful. If this occurs, then the infant must deal with an unhealthy level of mistrust that will affect all future relationships that call for trust, particularly her ability to trust God.

The virtue that can arise if faith is nurtured is hope. What is implied here is not necessarily hope for any particular thing but hope itself, or the ability to be a hopeful person. What does it mean to be hopeful? Hope includes anticipation, expectation, aspiration, and desire. Infants gain a stance in the world that hopes all things. Here is the basis for the ability to make personal faith commitments later in life. Without hope we have nothing. And this is the opposite or the weakness derived if nurture is neglected. The infant will instead have a sense of withdrawal or despondency and will not hope or anticipate; she will find trusting God difficult.

The ritualization of the infant is what Erikson refers to as the numinous. This refers to the aspects of relating that give to infants their pre-images of God. Parents' relationships with them give infants a sense of what it is to be in relationship with God. Obviously, this can be good or bad, nurturing or neglecting. If overdependency develops, then infants may develop the weakness of idolism. This is a way of relating that places too much trust on the parents and leads to an inability to recognize the limits of that relationship.

Thinking does occur in infancy. Many have denied this due to the absence of language skills; however, if thinking is making sense of the environment, then thinking occurs. Piaget refers to thinking in infancy as sensorimotor. All one need do is observe infants and watch how many things go in their mouths or how often they drop things to hear them as they hit the ground. They are getting to know things by way of their senses: sight, sound, taste, smell, and touch.

Childhood: Enculturating and Training versus Ignoring

The task of Christian formation between the ages of five and eleven is to enculturate and train children in the basic story of Christian faith. To enculturate is to pass on to children the particular ways in which we believe and live. This must not be done in a way that is abusive and authoritarian. John Westerhoff correctly points out the distinction between socialization and enculturation.[5] Socialization implies that someone is doing something to another without necessarily considering the rightness of the behavior; in a sense he is violating the other's personhood. Enculturation is introducing children into the mores and ways of the community of faith. It includes training in which we assist children in the practice of the rituals of Christian faith.

Using the word *training* indicates that this is not an appropriate time for reflective education. Children are not ready for reflecting on the value of particular rituals and beliefs, and we must have enough confidence in our own ways of being Christian that we carefully train children in these ways. We must also keep in mind that there will come a time when we must encourage reflection on these ways of being Christian. Ways of being Christian include the basic story of

5. John H. Westerhoff III, *Will Our Children Have Faith?* (New York: Seabury, 1976).

Christian faith and the language, rituals, and behaviors we employ to remind ourselves of it. Our task is to pass on these ways or face the possibility of our children's being ignorant of them. If we ignore them, our children will be ignorant of them. They will not know what the story of Christian faith is or how to behave in the community of faith. This ignorance will lead to a deficit for further Christian formation.

The cycle of enculturating and training versus ignoring incorporates two of the psychosocial stages of Erikson. For ages two through five, Erikson identifies the stage of autonomy versus shame and doubt, and for ages six through eleven, the stage of initiative versus guilt. It is interesting to watch the shift in religious understanding and expression between these two periods. David Elkind calls the religion of the earlier stage spontaneous and that of the later stage acquired. Younger children are free in their thinking and give fascinating responses to questions about religion. Older children have, by virtue of their religious training, acquired the "right answers" to many questions. Consider the story of the Sunday school teacher posing a question to her class: "Children, what is furry, grey, and has a long bushy tail?" After a long silence one brave child speaks up: "I know the answer is Jesus but it sure sounds like a squirrel to me!" Acquired religion at its best understands that in a majority of cases the correct answer in Sunday school is "Jesus."

Let us now consider the early years of this cycle, years Erikson labels as the stage of autonomy versus shame and doubt. By *autonomy* Erikson implies the ability of children to control themselves. As they acquire a variety of motor skills, a new sense of well-being comes about. My five-year-old daughter has, as of two days ago, begun to ride a bicycle. A few days ago I felt as if she would never be able to ride; I was exasperated in my attempts to help her. The moment she sensed the feeling of balance, her riding skills were in place. Now I watch in amazement as she turns quickly, uses her brakes, and rejoices in her new-found autonomy. She does not need Mom or Dad to hold her any longer.

Elkind points out that in adulthood "the sense of autonomy appears as a healthy sense of independence, a willingness to take a stand and to take responsibility for one's beliefs and actions."[6] This is clearly within the trajectory that is set for maturing Christian faith.

6. David Elkind, *Miseducation: Preschoolers at Risk* (New York: Alfred A. Knopf, 1987), p. 105.

The danger is the lack of autonomy that is described as shame and doubt. Shame is the feeling persons have when they have been totally exposed to the ridicule of others. They have been shown to be unable to control themselves, which leads to self-doubt and inability to attempt independent action. In adulthood this will probably, if uncorrected, produce persons who are unable to act independently and, in fact, will act legalistically. Their Christian faith will be understood or expressed not as a liberating part of their lives but as a restricting and shaming element that only controls them.

The virtue that comes about from the positive resolution of this stage is will. Erikson defines will as "the unbroken determination to exercise free choice as well as self-restraint."[7] Children can gain the virtue of self-responsibility, which is essential to a maturing Christian faith. However, if they are unable to resolve this stage positively, they will carry the vice of compulsion. Compulsion is an irresistible impulse to perform an irrational act. It is associated with obsessive behavior and feelings, which are irrational. If this becomes a part of the child's sense of self, then the dangers for Christian formation are clear. Here are the seeds of persons who, as adult Christians, live out their faith in obsessive and compulsive ways. They sense not liberation but enslavement. Their faith is driven by the letter of the law, not the spirit. Clearly, this is not part of a maturing Christian faith.

In terms of the ritualizations and ritualisms of this stage, we find more that relates to this compulsivity. Erikson finds the ritualization of "judicious" relationships and the ritualism of "legalistic" relationships. The tension is between the ability to be willful and self-responsible in relationships and the danger of being compulsive and legalistic. This shapes the way one relates both to other people and to God.

Cognitively, this stage is wonderful. Piaget refers to the thinking at this stage as pre-operational. It precedes the ability to work logically with ideas. Children in this stage are unable to carry out operations or follow the steps of solving a problem. Their ability to understand the order of events is weak, as are their abilities to explain cause and effect and to understand rules. The joy of this stage is the free-associating, imaginative thinking that they exhibit. At this age, imagination is at its best. There is a fantasy level to all thinking. In relationship to faith this has a sometimes disquieting effect for adults. Children typically make no distinction between Jesus and Superman

7. Erik H. Erikson, *Insight and Responsibility* (New York: Norton, 1964), p. 119.

or Santa Claus. There may even be a bias toward Santa Claus, since at least once a year children feel tangible evidence of his existence.

Fowler says that the faith of this age is intuitive, guided by hunches, not logic. This creates the impression that children of this age are profoundly insightful about theological issues. In one of the courses I teach, an assignment is to interview persons from a variety of ages. After one student had interviewed five-year-olds, he voiced his amazement at one child's grasp of the nature of the Trinity. For this child there was no problem thinking that God the Father and Jesus were two separate persons yet one God. What the student failed to realize was that the complexity of the issue was not even accessible to the child. The child was simply "free thinking" and imagining that anything was possible.

The next psychosocial stage in this cycle is that of initiative versus guilt. It includes the years from six through eleven. As Erikson states, "Initiative adds to autonomy the quality of undertaking, planning and 'attacking' a task for the sake of being active."[8] This implies the ability to take initiative in beginning and completing projects. Are children willing to take risks? Are they willing to attempt new tasks and make new friendships? I think again of my daughter's attempts at bike riding. Once she decided she wanted to ride, there was no stopping her. She took the initiative and stuck with the task until she mastered it. The opposing tension at this stage is guilt or inhibition. This implies the feeling that one has gone too far, has overextended her initiative. This is most apparent in making new friends. Children are often hurt when other children ask them to stay away, possibly because they have imposed themselves too often. Children may then become more inhibited than is healthy. They may fear attempting new tasks or friendships. Clearly, inhibition is one vice that needs to be present in small amounts. We must be aware that we can over-step the limits of tasks or relationships.

The virtue of this stage is purpose. This is something like the courage to pursue goals. It is determination that I can and will attack something and achieve a valued end. The fear is the lack of purpose and determination that Erikson again calls inhibition. Children who lack purpose will find it difficult to make friends and achieve success in school.

Erikson calls the ritualization element of this stage the dramatic. This is the play age, when children love to act. Humor is becoming a

8. Erik H. Erikson, *Childhood and Society* (New York: Norton, 1950), p. 255.

part of their lives. They enjoy the Christmas pageants and their parts in them. The contrasting fear is a ritualism characterized by moralism. This is a suppression of the dramatic play due to inhibitions about oneself. Undoubtedly, unhealthy inhibitions have stifled many a budding actor or actress. Cognitively, children of this age may enter the stage of concrete operations. They learn to do logical operations. This implies that they understand cause-and-effect relationships and hold events in order of occurrence. The limitation is that thought is limited to real, concrete persons, objects, and experiences.

The psychosocial strength of initiative and the desire to dramatize life combined with concrete operations yields a love for story. "The distinctive new strength of this stage," writes Walter Conn, "is the ability to narratize experience. In contrast to younger children who must depend on stories told by others, the preadolescent with concrete operations has the capacity to generate his or her own stories."[9] This new-found strength is tempered by the limitations of concreteness. This often leads to an anthropomorphic view of God, that is, the necessity of God's having concrete form and presence.

Fowler rightly characterizes this age with a faith development stage named mythic-literal. All stories of faith are literalized so as to make sense. Elkind points out that children of this age often draw pictures of priests or ministers to concretize God. A story may illustrate. Tyron was a six-year-old attending a vacation Bible school of which I was director. His teacher mentioned to me that Tyron had accepted Jesus into his heart and that it might be helpful if I encouraged him. I did so, and here is how the conversation went:

"Tyron, I hear you accepted Jesus into your heart?"

"Yeah, that's right and it's great!"

"Where is Jesus now?" (My attempt to test his orthodoxy!)

"In my heart."

"How do you know Jesus is in your heart?"

"Oh, he came in my nose, in my mouth, through my ears. He's in my heart cause I can feel him—I'm a bit sore but I think I'll be ok."

The effects of concrete operations are clear!

Another effect of this age is the confusion that arises over theology. The profound grasp of the Trinity found in the five-year-old now gives way to a futile attempt to make sense out of a two-in-one God—let alone three. When children are asked about the Trinity

9. Walter Conn, *Christian Conversion: A Developmental Interpretation of Autonomy and Surrender* (Mahwah, N.J.: Paulist, 1986), p. 46.

they typically give the "acquired" response, which tends to satisfy the inquirer. If, however, you pursue the issue, you will soon find confusion as they attempt to figure out how God the Father and Jesus can have been one while Jesus was on earth and the Father was in heaven.

In summary, the cycle of enculturating/training versus ignoring is a time for forming in children their first appreciation for the story of the gospel. There is the opportunity early on to capitalize on the imagination and then on the storying ability of children. Psychosocially, many of the cornerstone issues related to a maturing faith are dealt with here. The early sense of trust is built on by adding autonomy, will, initiative, purpose, and determination. These contribute to a maturing faith that is liberating instead of restrictive. The two psychosocial crises within the cycle of nurturing and enculturating make up the childhood years. On these foundations the possibility of a firm faith is built. As Fowler states, "The quality of mutuality and the strength of trust, autonomy, hope and courage (or their opposites) developed in this phase underlie (or threaten to undermine) all that comes later in faith development."[10]

---

10. James W. Fowler, *Stages of Faith: The Psychology of Human Development and the Quest for Meaning* (New York: Harper & Row, 1981), p. 121.

11

Cycles of Christian Formation in Adolescence

The adolescent years are divided into three stages: early adolescence (11–14), middle adolescence (15–17), and late adolescence (18–25). These generalizations group together ages that tend to experience similar issues, and there is much overlap between the issues of various age periods. We must also remember that persons are individuals and travel their own life journeys that may or may not correspond with the generalizations. The adolescent years incorporate two of the cycles of Christian formation: belonging versus alienation and searching versus entrenchment.

Belonging versus Alienation

In early adolescence, the sense of wanting to belong becomes stronger than ever. Adolescents are looking for a group of peers and significant others that affirms them as belonging to it. John Westerhoff calls this affiliative faith. The task of the faith community is to give to adolescents a sense of belonging. This can be difficult due to the apparent lack of interest in organized religion at this age.[1]

If adolescents do not develop a sense of belonging, then they will feel alienated—withdrawn or estranged. It can also imply the with-

1. Information from LEAP (Listening to Early Adolescents and Their Parents) Project report published in 1984 by the SEARCH Institute, 122 West Franklin Ave., Minneapolis, MN, 55404.

drawal of affection or a sense of belonging that was previously offered by significant others. This means that alienation has both implicit and explicit dimensions. One can be alienated subtly by quiet exclusion or more overtly by outright rejection. It appears that this age is one in which both of these forms of alienation occur.

I remember the sorrow a colleague of mine felt as he recalled what had happened to his thirteen-year-old daughter. She had been close friends with two other girls and had done many things with them, one of which was shopping. The problem arose when she discovered by accident that the other two had made shopping plans and excluded her. When she contacted them to find out when they were going, assuming the exclusion was by accident, she was told that she was not invited. The pain of exclusion and alienation runs deep. In these cases the faith community can do little, but it does have a responsibility to educate early adolescents with a sense of inclusion. Adolescents without a sense of belonging will feel alienated from friends, the church, and possibly God. How can the church work toward creating a sense of belonging in early adolescence?

Industry and Competency

Erik Erikson suggests that we create a sense of industry and competency in the early adolescent. People who feel as if they have something to offer a group will feel as if they belong to it. We all want to feel as if we can make a contribution to those who are important to us. The sense of industry means we have a "sense of being useful."[2] It is the desire to make things and do things well. It includes the development of workmanship, promptness, neatness, and care. As David Elkind puts it, it is "confidence in our knowledge, skills, and talents and our ability to put them into practice."[3] Early adolescents need to learn the things that will make them productive citizens in their culture. For the church this means learning things that will help adolescents on their way in a maturing faith. The negative side of this is the possibility that early adolescents will develop a sense not of industry but of inferiority and inadequacy. They sense that there is nothing they can do well, nothing they can contribute to their

2. Erik H. Erikson, *Identity and the Life Cycle: Selected Papers* (New York: Norton, 1980), p. 91.
3. David Elkind, *Miseducation: Preschoolers at Risk* (New York: Alfred A. Knopf, 1987), p. 137.

group. Without the sense of industry one will get "the feeling that one will never be any good."[4] Early adolescents may find themselves not knowing the enjoyment of work and the "pride of doing at least one kind of thing well."[5]

Erikson claims that the resulting virtue of a positive resolution of this stage leads to a sense of competency. "Competence, then, is the free exercise of dexterity and intelligence in the completion of tasks. . . ."[6] Here is the freedom and desire to do things and to do them well. In the context of the church it implies that early adolescents have the freedom and desire to "show their stuff." That is, the church celebrates all of the things they can do. If it is totally unrelated to the church, adolescents still can do their thing and receive praise.

More particularly, adolescents can feel free and pleased to practice the skills of Christian formation. I recall the importance of my home church allowing me as a young adolescent to read Scripture in worship and to perform duties for the church that were related to budding areas of competency.

The negative pole is a sense of inertia. This means both a lack of skill and a lack of motion. Not only do young adolescents feel inadequate, they also develop this vice of inertia. They feel as if they have nothing to contribute, so they don't. They remain motionless, as it were, because they feel as if they can't go anywhere anyway.

The resulting ritualization is the sense of the formal or the technical. Early adolescents begin to relate to others and to one another in ways that are directly related to the idea of meaningful work and contribution. They begin to relate in ways that reflect a sense of worth based on their being accepted as contributing to their group, so they feel good about what they have to offer. In contrast, the early adolescent with no sense of belonging due to a feeling of incompetence may relate to others and perform tasks in a stiff, legalistic fashion. This is the ritualism of formalism. It is the danger of perfectionism and stiff legalism. Donald Capps calls it "an excessive reliance on proficiency for proficiency's sake."[7] Capps indicates that in the church this is exemplified in empty ceremonialism. We perform duties of worship in meaningless ways. We perform our own

4. Erikson, *Identity and the Life Cycle,* p. 92.

5. Ibid., p. 93.

6. Erik H. Erikson, *Insight and Responsibility* (New York: Norton, 1964), p. 124.

7. Donald Capps, *Life Cycle Theory and Pastoral Care* (Philadelphia: Fortress, 1983), p. 67.

spiritual disciplines in repetitious, empty ways. Why? Because we are supposed to! Why? Because we have always done it that way! Indeed, Christian formation can be harmed at this point if we do not take care to work toward a sense of industry and competency that yields meaningful habits of work and a sense of belonging. We can end up having early adolescents feeling alienated, with nothing to contribute to the life of the church and no sense of freedom and joy in the spiritual disciplines.

Cognitive Development

Cognitively, one of the major revolutions in thinking is occurring here that will lead to maturing Christian faith. It is the development of ability to do formal operations. "Formal operations provide thinking with an entirely new ability that detaches and liberates thinking from concrete reality and permits it to build its own reflections and theories," writes Jean Piaget. "With the advent of formal intelligence, thinking takes wings, and it is not surprising that at first this unexpected power is both used and abused."[8] Formal operations includes thinking about possibilities, thinking through hypotheses, thinking ahead, and thinking about thoughts.[9] It is this thinking that brings about the ability to realize that persons have opinions about others.

Elkind points out four results of this new ability. First, it can bring about what he calls pseudostupidity: "Young adolescents often appear stupid because they are, in fact, too bright."[10] What Elkind means is that they will often apply formal operations to tasks that do not require them. This can become annoying to parents and others who work with early adolescents. Second, the advent of formal operations may lead them to exhibit apparent hypocrisy. This is an effect of their inability to link grand ideals with actual behavior. How often have we heard the grand plans of a vibrant Christian life following an emotional camp experience, then seen Christian teenagers return home, still espousing the ideals of love and commitment, and scream

8. Jean Piaget, *Six Psychological Studies*, ed. David Elkind (New York: Random House, 1968), pp. 63, 64.

9. Daniel Keating, "Thinking Processes in Adolescence," in *Handbook of Adolescent Psychology*, ed. Joseph Adelson (New York: Wiley, 1980), pp. 212–15.

10. David Elkind, "Understanding the Young Adolescent," in *The Life Cycle: Readings in Human Development*, ed. Lawrence D. Steinberg (New York: Columbia University Press, 1982), p. 169.

at their brothers or sisters and fail to complete even the smallest task of love? They truly mean their commitments, yet behavior and practice are miles apart from their ideals, as they are in all of us.

Third, there is the personal fable. This is the belief that the adolescent is not subject to what all others are subject to, or that no one else experiences what he does. This may be found in early adolescents who confide in a parent that they have been dumped by a true love and that the parent simply cannot know the pain involved, since she has never been in love. Or it may be seen in young adolescents who behave recklessly simply because they do not believe that whatever happens to others can also happen to them.

Finally, this stage brings the imaginary audience. The development of the ability to think about others' thinking leads to an inability to separate what they are actually thinking from what we imagine they are thinking, particularly about ourselves. This results in the hyper self-consciousness of early adolescents. This is why belonging becomes so important. Now, more than ever before, they are aware of their own and others' hidden thoughts that result in their feeling accepted or rejected.

Christian Formation

In terms of understanding biblical and theological issues, formal operations bring both potentials and problems. The potential is that early adolescents can now see themselves in the story of faith rather than just know the story of faith. The problems arise in that if a too rigid and too literalistic understanding of faith has been enculturated in early adolescents, they may feel duped or betrayed as they come to initial recognition of some of the complexities of faith. This is what led Ronald Goldman to recommend that little if any religious education should be done prior to adolescence.[11]

Summarizing, the cycle of belonging versus alienation is the time when early adolescents are attempting to find something that they can do so as to feel competent and have a basis for belonging to a group. The new abilities in cognitive development lead to new possibilities for Christian formation. The task of educational ministry is to find ways to assist early adolescents in becoming competent Christians and in finding a place to belong.

11. See Ronald Goldman, *Readiness for Religion* (New York: Seabury, 1968), pp. 75–80.

Searching versus Entrenchment

Identity Formation

"The search is what anyone would undertake if he were not sunk in the everydayness of his own life."[12] So says Walker Percy of life in general, but it is also true of life in Christian faith. We can become comfortable and avoid the hard work necessary to continue maturing in faith. Once a level of belonging is achieved, however, it is time to search out all the aspects of one's faith. Gordon Allport believes that "commencing in later childhood or adolescence the individual who is on the way to maturity probably will repudiate both the oversimplified product of his earlier egocentric thinking, and blind conformity to institutional or parental views."[13] For some, searching may seem counterproductive to Christian formation, but it is essential if people are to come into a maturing Christian faith.

This cycle is divided into two parts: initial searching and searching. Initial searching includes the high school years, in which adolescents may or may not be actively searching their faith but are involved in searching out other aspects of their lives and will, soon enough, include faith in the search. There is still a strong urge on the part of adolescents to belong: witness the typical high school church camp closing service, which is usually a fireside service at which emotions are flowing. Everyone loves everyone and is *so* glad to be part of such a loving group!

The "soon enough" of the search generally comes around age nineteen. This can create a whole new way of seeing life, particularly if older adolescents attend college. The danger is that they will not begin the search and will continue in a second-hand faith or in an "everyday faith."

Psychosocially, this cycle begins with identity versus identity confusion. Erikson is concerned about two key ingredients in identity. First, identity is not simply the accumulation of identifications from childhood, so that people become some composite of these identifications. Identity "is more than the sum of the childhood identifications."[14] This illustrates the active quality of identity formation, which may take hold of or reject identifications from parents and

12. Walker Percy, *The Moviegoer* (New York: Ballantine, 1960), p. 9.
13. Gordon Allport, *The Individual and His Religion* (New York: Macmillan, 1957), p. 68.
14. Erikson, *Identity and the Life Cycle,* p. 94.

others who have had significance for adolescents. Second, there is the need for a sense of self-sameness. What is being sought is a centering of self so that adolescents know who they are no matter what setting they find themselves in. Adolescents also need others to confirm their self-sameness. "Do you see me as I see myself? Do you see me as the same self in different situations?" Identity is also formed as adolescents choose values and an occupation. What is the adolescent going to value? What will she do in life?

The negative side of the crisis is that adolescents may be unable to resolve the confusion over who they are, to select or reject from the identification choices before them. They may not be able to gain a sense of self-sameness. This typically manifests itself in what Elkind calls the "patchwork self." By this he means individuals who cannot decide what centers them. This is most evident when adolescents change dramatically depending upon what group they are with. This may be called a chameleon identity. It occurs when we change identities to match the groups we are with. It happens to us all in the process of identity formation, but it becomes a sign of identity confusion if self-sameness is not established eventually. Confusion also reveals itself in the inability to say no. Adolescents who do not have a sense of identity do not have a value system from which to judge situations. They also tend to be unable to make occupational choices, an inability that immobilizes them.

The virtue arising from identity formation is fidelity. Fidelity is a sense of loyalty and duty, of being true and authentic. If identity is formed with fidelity, the individual can gain a keen sense of well-being. Fidelity is essential to maturing faith. In order to be a maturing Christian one must be loyal, faithful, and authentic.

The vice is role repudiation. This is the active rejection of any identity choices, thereby rendering adolescents untrue and inauthentic. They are unwilling to take on any identity, and this unwillingness is active.

The ritualization here is ideological. Adolescents use rites to develop a sense of belonging to the group. The high school pep rally comes to mind, or the football team breaking through the paper banner after halftime. These rites affirm adolescents' togetherness. The danger is totalism. This is adolescents' fanatic and excessive involvement in what their peers deem right. Nothing else matters to them and they become consumed by their ideology. This is why cult groups attract adolescents with fragile identities. They provide an outlet for excessive and fanatic commitment.

Each of these psychosocial issues helps to make this age the period with the most religious conversions. The typical age for conversion is sixteen. Adolescents, in their attempts to form their identities, can turn to the gospel and find something to be devoted to, something that shapes their values and provides a context for self-sameness. Care must be taken not to offer an illegitimate notion of conversion to adolescents. Often we offer conversion as a once-and-for-all fix-all. This is a disservice and does not convey the reality of Christian conversion, which is only the beginning. But again, conversion is an act of centering the person, which is what identity formation is about.

Cognitively, people in this stage begin to generalize formal oper-ations. Adolescents become more skillful in formal thinking, over-coming the problems of initial formal operations. The limits here are that thinking is probably dualistic. It is formal, but it sees all issues as either right or wrong, good or bad. This exhibits itself in adolescents finding heroes to follow. As Fowler would state, this is a conform-ing stage in faith. Adolescents look to authority figures and cannot critique them.

The identity quest comes to the forefront during initial searching. In this time, adolescents may not be ready to search their faith, but the search is on in their lives. It is a time to assist them in identity formation, which is in fact a way of assisting them in their process of Christian formation.

The search comes to full speed in the late teens and early twen-ties, when many Americans are in college and have more freedom than ever to try on identities and explore options. James Marcia has explored typical ways in which adolescents work through the iden-tity crisis.[15] He identifies four identity statuses: identity diffused, identity foreclosed, identity moratorium, and identity achieved. He assesses these through an interview that asks about adolescents' views on politics, religion, and occupation. On each of these the researcher listens for responses that reflect the presence or absence of crises and commitments. A crisis is described as an active search for a position or for an answer to an issue. A commitment is a stance on an issue. Adolescents described as identity diffused would give no indication of either crisis or commitment. Identity-foreclosed adolescents would not exhibit crisis but would have made commitments. Iden-

15. See James Marcia, "Identity in Adolescence," in *Handbook of Adolescent Psy-chology*, pp. 159–87.

tity moratorium people would have crises but no commitments, and identity-achieved people would have both crises and commitments. Typically, the eighteen- to twenty-year-old is in identity moratorium. She is pursuing questions about occupation, values, religion, politics, and relationships. Often she is so busy with these issues that she has little time for anything else. She exhibits few signs of commitment but many signs of tentativeness and change. It is quite fair to ask, "What are your commitments today?" This is a healthy condition for older adolescents, although they and their parents do not think so. These are the years when the search is most active.

One reason why these years seem most fertile for the birth of identity is that adolescents are leaving home. Here is their chance to attempt to be autonomous from their parents. This typically creates what Sharon Parks terms "counter-dependence," in which adolescents push off from adult authority. It is not necessarily a reactionary move but one in which adolescents are saying, "Let me try it myself." This brings on good feelings of independence and freedom as well as feelings of fear and vulnerability.

These years also bring an active idealism. As Parks states, "A central strength of the young adult is the capacity to respond to visions of the world as it might become."[16] I recall a sophomore student speaking to me about his guilt feelings for spending time studying when there was so much to be done. He felt as if he should quit college and go serve the poor somewhere. His visions were honorable, his timing a bit off.

It is true that many choose not to attend college, and this will affect the development of their faith. If it goes the way of most other areas of life, such as views on politics and morality, then we can speculate that the faith of non-college attenders will eventually change in the same direction as college attenders. This change, however, will be slower, which may keep it from occurring at all.

Intimate Relationships

Complicating the resolution of identity are questions of relationships. Here and on into young adulthood the crisis of intimacy versus isolation comes to ascendancy. The primary discussion of this crisis will be in the next cycle of faith, but aspects of it need to be addressed here.

16. Sharon Parks, *The Critical Years* (New York: Harper & Row, 1986), p. 98.

Research on identity formation shows an important difference in how males and females resolve the identity question. Studies of identity statuses, in particular, create problems when we look at gender differences. Females do not work through identity issues in the same way as males. Most psychological studies are subtly biased toward men in how they describe the identity search. Women *seem* to forestall identity resolution until questions of relationships can be included.[17] This may be the case, or the research may have failed to pay sufficient attention to the issue of relationships for men. Whatever the case, women are more concerned with relationships than men, and this influences the course of identity development. This also affects how men work through their identity issues. They should pay more attention to relationships and their effect on identity.

When I ask college students, both male and female, to identify which of the Eriksonian stages they think they are working through, invariably the response is both identity and intimacy. As one student put it, "Just when I think I have some clue as to my identity, then I become involved in a relationship that sends me running back to identity issues. The opposite is also true. I find that I can't really think about my identity without also thinking about those who are closest to me." This answer happened to come from a male student who voiced what many college-age students are experiencing.

Cognitive Development

William Perry traced cognitive development in the college years and identified a three-level, nine-position scheme.[18] The three levels include dualism, which is black-and-white thinking; multiplism, which is best understood as a type of uncritical relativism; and commitment in relativism, which understands the complexity of reality yet also recognizes the necessity of critiquing competing positions and taking a stand with incomplete information. Most freshmen going to college exhibit dualistic thinking. They look for the correct answer and get frustrated when a professor "pretends" not to have it.

The move to multiplism is difficult and is best described by the phrase "you can't go home again." College students begin to real-

17. See Marcia, "Identity in Adolescence." See also S. Ginsburg and J. Orlofsky, "Ego Identity Status, Ego Development, and Locus of Control in College Women," *Journal of Youth and Adolescence* 10 (August 1981): 297–307.

18. William Perry, *Forms of Intellectual and Ethical Development in the College Years* (New York: Holt, Rinehart and Winston, 1970).

ize that life is not so simple and the answers are not all clear. In so doing they may be moving away from positions held by parents and significant others in their lives.

Finally, if they have mentors to guide their development, they may come to commitment in relativism: the ability to take stands in the midst of uncertainty. "One discovers that there is a difference between just any opinion and an opinion that is grounded in careful and thoughtful observation and reflection," writes Parks.[19] Commitment in relativism is also the ability to consider alternate viewpoints critically.

Christian Formation

What do these cognitive and psychosocial issues have to say to Christian formation? If identity and cognition are undergoing major transformations, then faith must be undergoing major transformations as well. The psychosocial and cognitive transformations are normative for human maturity. The related changes in faith are also essential for maturing faith. Older adolescents have the potential to form a new faith, but they run the risk of settling for an immature faith. This becomes a crucial period in the formation of Christian faith. Previously, individuals had little choice about the changes that would occur. Now they can see the changes coming—not clearly, but they can see them. This may lead them to reject the changes and settle in or become entrenched. "At this period of development," writes Allport, "the youth is compelled to transform his religious attitudes—indeed all his attitudes—from second-hand fittings to first-hand fittings of his personality."[20] Or, as Parks puts it, "To arrive at true faith, one must first pass through a stage of unbelief."[21] A period of active searching is essential to maturing faith.

Older adolescents begin the search with a faith that was sufficient up to this point but no longer is. Theirs is a conformist faith that seeks to fulfill the expectations of significant others. This was fine when identity was absorbed in the group to which one belonged, but it is not useful for persons who have developed some initial sense of their own identity. Immature faith is conformist and dualistic. According to Parks, "People who compose self, world, and 'God' in this form can make clear divisions between what is true and untrue,

19. Parks, *The Critical Years*, p. 50.
20. Allport, *The Individual and His Religion*, p. 36.
21. Parks, *The Critical Years*, p. 191.

right and wrong, 'we' and 'they.' There is little or no tolerance for ambiguity."[22] These individuals who refuse to begin or continue the search often couch their immaturity in spiritual language. "It is not spiritual to question." "One must believe those whom God has placed over us." Or, as Daniel Helminiak puts it, "Too intent on becoming 'spiritual,' they follow the master, keep the rules, affirm the teachings, all without question or responsible criticism."[23] What is particularly distressful is that the church in general seems to feed on the conformist mindset, whether the church is theologically liberal or conservative. Walter Brueggemann speaks of "fake evangelicalism" that speaks with "shameless certitude" and ignores the tough questions of life. Indeed, Laurent Daloz states that a chief function of fundamentalistic thinking is to "keep information manageable and reduce painful ambiguity."[24] This conformity, need for certainty, and lack of tolerance for ambiguity are characteristic of those who have ignored or shut out the search. Their faith will remain immature until they are willing to understand that doubt is the seed of faith. This is entrenching faith.

The question remains, then, "What is the task of the search and how does it look and feel?" The task is to stand against the faith as given in order to test and critique it. It is a task of making Christian faith owned. The feelings associated with the search range from exhilaration to deep fear. We become excited to realize that we have a faith of our own and that God loves us in the midst of our questions. However, "when we undergo the shipwreck of meaning at the level of faith, we feel threatened at the very core of our existence."[25] There is the fear that we have gone too far, that we have questioned too much, or that our parents and our faith communities may reject and not understand us. This raises doubts about the legitimacy of the search. "Maybe they are right. If the search is to lead to mature faith, then why are so many people rejecting me?" Ecclesiastes 1:18 says that with much knowledge comes much grief. That is true. But with much knowledge also comes the responsibility to shape it into a mature faith. So arise fear, doubt, a sense of tentativeness. Persons in the midst of the search do not believe anything too much! They

22. Ibid., p. 45.

23. Daniel A. Helminiak, *Spiritual Development: An Introductory Study* (Chicago: Loyola University Press, 1987), p. 78.

24. Laurent Daloz, *Effective Teaching and Mentoring: Realizing the Transformational Power of Adult Learning Experiences* (San Francisco: Jossey-Bass, 1986), p. 148.

25. Parks, *The Critical Years*, p. 24.

are fearful that they might be wrong, as they were before. They are in a moratorium of faith. But this exploration of faith is needed, for out of it comes the discovery of a newly found maturing faith. As Daloz states, "Our old life is still there, but its meaning has profoundly changed because we have left home, seen it from afar, and been transformed by that vision."[26]

From early to late adolescence the tasks of Christian formation are to develop a sense of belonging to the Christian community and to search in order to own one's faith. These tasks can be assisted along the way if the faith community helps adolescents to develop a sense of competence and identity.

---

26. Daloz, *Effective Teaching and Mentoring,* p. 26.

12

Cycles of Christian Formation in Adulthood

Consolidation versus Fragmentation

In my younger days I spent a good deal of time canoeing down rivers. Often we would take on rapids. I recall the excitement as we heard the roar of the upcoming rapids and prepared to be in the proper position in the river as we entered them. Then we paddled frantically. Once in the rapids the job was to keep the canoe straight and avoid the rocks. Typically, it was not long until we left the rapids and reached calm, tranquil waters. Then we bailed out water, checked our gear, and reordered ourselves in preparation for the next rapids. We could do this without paying too much attention to the river because there were always eddies of calm water without any current in which we could rest.

The cycle of consolidation versus fragmentation is like that. Coming out of the rapid and disorienting pace of searching faith, we enter a calm in which we can put things in order. It could be described as a period of latency in Christian formation. Often we hear criticism of the radicals of the 1960s. "Where are they now? Working in the banks they burned! Wearing suits and power ties and 'doing' lunch! Not having a critical word about the government! At home fertilizing the yard and changing diapers!" These comments are meant to be a judgment on the apparent lack of consistency between the radicals' former countercultural lives and their present common lives. The problem is that the critics miss the deeper issues of the life cycle.

155

In relation to Christian formation, the issues are similar. Often those who were most involved in the search during adolescence are now tending to the practicalities of life. Friends may look at them and say, "Weren't you the campus heretic?" Those issues seem to have disappeared beneath the stacks of bills, classified ads, and diapers. When adults at midlife are asked to think about their formation as Christians, they refer to the search during adolescence, then describe young adulthood as something like "getting on with it" or "a water stop."

There is a season for everything, including our maturing faith. An old Zen saying states, "After the enlightenment, the laundry." We need a season to pull together the practicalities of life—to consolidate. The danger is that we will not consolidate with faith at the center of our decisions. We may unknowingly make decisions about a variety of issues that subtly move us from the faith we had searched out in late adolescence. Of course, this assumes that the previous cycle included the search and not entrenchment. If entrenchment came before, faith will continue on its simple, unreflective way.

We turn now to a description of the psychosocial, cognitive, and Christian formation issues embedded in this cycle of consolidation versus fragmentation.

Love and Work

It is said that Sigmund Freud once was asked to describe mature adult life. His response was supposedly, "*Lieben und arbeiten.*" To love and to work. Whether the story is true or not, the response is useful. The main issues of young adulthood are love and work.

Erik Erikson refers to the psychosocial crisis of this period as intimacy versus isolation. This crisis begins in late adolescence but is now at full ascendancy. George Vaillant states that for the men in his study this period provided a time where "wives were wooed and won, and friendships that were to endure into adulthood deepened."[1] Erikson states that the young adult is "ready for intimacy, that is, the capacity to commit himself to concrete affiliations and partnerships and to develop the ethical strength to abide by such commitments, even though they may call for significant sacrifices and compromises."[2] He insists that only those who have developed some sort of a solid identity can risk that identity in relationships.

1. George E. Vaillant, *Adaptation to Life* (Boston: Little, Brown, 1977), p. 215.
2. Erik H. Erikson, *Childhood and Society* (New York: Norton, 1950), p. 263.

Intimacy refers to deep and lasting relationships that individuals develop. These relationships can be with a marriage partner, class friends and mentors, or colleagues in the work place. They are not superficial relationships that seek only to "network" so as to use others for one's own gain. They may exact large costs for the individual.

The negative pole of this crisis is isolation, or as Erikson puts it, "the counterpart of intimacy is distantiation: the readiness to isolate and, if necessary, to destroy those forces and people whose essence seems dangerous to one's own."[3] Persons may be unable to give themselves in relationships and therefore become threatened by them, so they withdraw and retreat from any interaction with others. The interaction that does go on is only what is necessary and self-serving. Self-isolating people get to know others only for their own benefit. Superficial relationships replace those of true intimacy in which we allow someone to know who we truly are. Sexual relations replace intimacy because we confuse sex with intimacy.

If, however, a positive resolution occurs, the virtue of love results. "Love, then, is mutuality of devotion forever subduing the antagonisms inherent in divided function."[4] Erikson's definition of love puts to rest any simple romantic notion of love that we may think comes with intimacy. Love requires mutuality. Much of what today's culture passes off as love is simply self-serving use of others. There is no sense that we are in relationships for the sake of the other as well as ourselves. Love also requires devotion, the act of costly commitment to someone else. And love is chosen and active. It does not simply happen to us; we must choose it. The vice opposed to love is exclusivity, or the inability to love. It is rejection of others and the denial of the human need for relationships.

Young adults attempting to develop intimacy obviously need to develop ways of being in relationship with others. The ritualization of this crisis is affiliation. By affiliation, Erikson implies that we desire to spend time with others as we work toward personal relationships. Young adults developing intimacy seek to be with others, to spend time together, whether an evening or a vacation. They also seek places where there are others like them. There is nothing wrong with this unless it is associated with the negative resolution of this crisis, which brings with it the ritualism of elitism, which Erikson says "cultivates all sorts of cliques and clans marked more by snobbery than

3. Ibid., p. 264.
4. Erik H. Erikson, *Insight and Responsibility* (New York: Norton, 1964), p. 129.

by a living style."[5] Those with whom we affiliate are those of like mind. Negatively, Erikson refers to this as "pseudospeciation," or the belief that all of humankind are or should be my kind. In the church this becomes ugly as those of different classes or cultures or ways of understanding the Christian faith reject one another. "Unless you live and act as I do, you are not Christian."

Intimacy brings the ability to be in relationship with others. This brings the virtue of love, which implies commitment. It also brings a style of living that exhibits a desire to be with others. Negatively, it may bring isolation, exclusivity, and elitism.

But love is only half of the equation for healthy adulthood. The other major factor in adults' lives is work. Vaillant writes, "Between Erikson's stage of Intimacy and his stage of Generativity appeared an intermediate stage of Career Consolidation—a time when they, like Shakespeare's soldier, sought 'the bauble Reputation'."[6] The young adult must find a way to meet the basic necessities of life. Typically no one wants just the basic necessities, so it means finding work that will lead to the type of life style they desire as well as being fulfilling and satisfying. For many, what they do defines who they are. This is obviously an over-commitment to work, but it exhibits the power of career consolidation in young adults. They tend to take on the life styles of their workmates; they dress alike and talk alike. They develop what Robert N. Bellah calls "lifestyle enclaves"—groups of like-minded people who affirm what each other are doing and in turn are affirmed.

What is interesting is that the issues of love and work conflict. The major obstacle to intimacy is work. It takes time away from spouse, family, and friends. It also fills the gap when there is a lack or loss of intimacy or a dissatisfaction with intimacy. At the same time, love gets in the way of fulfilling one's aspirations for work. Relationships keep us from seventy- to eighty-hour work weeks and possibly from climbing the career ladder. What is needed is some way to consciously orchestrate the development of both.

Daniel J. Levinson refers to this as building an adult life structure. He sees young adulthood as the novice phase of adulthood.[7] The tasks here are to form an occupation, relationships, a dream of adult

5. Erik H. Erikson, *The Life Cycle Completed: A Review* (New York: Norton, 1982), p. 72.

6. Vaillant, *Adaptation to Life*, p. 202.

7. Daniel J. Levinson, et al., *The Seasons of a Man's Life* (New York: Ballantine, 1978).

life, and a mentor relationship that will assist in bringing the dream to life, and to choose a life style and values. There is also a tension between settling down and moving on. If we settle in, then we may miss a good career option. If we take the career move, we may harm relationships. The dream is one's vision of her future life. It directs decisions and empowers action. The mentor is someone who believes in the person and assists her in living toward the dream. All of these issues of the life structure have considerable impact on Christian formation, to which we will turn shortly.

Cognitive Development

Before considering the specifics of Christian formation, however, something must be said of cognitive development in this period. It appears that formal operations are done in either a dichotomizing or a dialectic fashion. Dichotomizing means something like dualistic thinking. Issues fall into neat, identifiable categories. If they do not, then something must be wrong. How often have we heard, "It's just too hard to understand, so it must be wrong"? This is particularly true when it comes to matters of Christian faith. The other option is dialectic thinking. This is more like the ability to hold two viewpoints in tension while considering the validity of each. It is what may be called divergent thinking, which acknowledges that there may be more than one right answer. Typical young adults, most likely due to the pressures of love and work, exhibit dichotomizing thinking. They tend not to be comfortable with opposing viewpoints or alternate ways of viewing issues.

A second issue related to cognition in young adulthood is the strength, and sometimes the weakness, of being able to view situations more realistically. "Adult knowing," says Walter Conn, "decenters the flighty, totalistic logic of adolescence by bringing it back to the earth of complex situations, where the idealism of simplistic certitude gives way to the realism of nuanced probability."[8] Again, this may be positive or negative. How often do we hear adolescents accuse adults of having lost all their ideals, or adults accusing adolescents of being naively optimistic and idealistic? The truth is, the complexity of surviving as an adult makes the highly idealistic answers of youth a bit less believable. Both might be correct, but one

8. Walter Conn, *Christian Conversion: A Developmental Interpretation of Autonomy and Surrender* (Mahwah, N.J.: Paulist, 1986), p. 56.

without the other is either overly idealistic or overly realistic. Young adults tend to become more realistic as they attempt to carve out their adult life structures.

Christian Formation

What does all of this tell us about the nature and tasks of Christian formation in young adulthood? Let us first discuss the nature of Christian formation. Vaillant says of the men in his study that in their early thirties they "seemed to be too busy becoming, too busy mastering crafts; too busy ascending prescribed career ladders to reflect upon their own vicissitudes of living."[9] In other words, the tasks of love and work tend to make latent the desire to reflect critically on one's life and faith. Persons may have been deeply reflective about faith in college but do not seem to find the time as young adults.

A former student of mine became involved in philosophy in college, and this led him to deep reflection on his faith. He went off to graduate school to work toward a masters in theology but found the program dissatisfying. When I asked what he would do, his response was that he was going to take a job and see what that was like. He had married just before leaving and wanted to spend some time getting his life together in regard to his marriage and job skills. Another student graduated and went off to teach in a private Christian school. In the face of some difficult situations he wrote, "Theology and philosophy and all my questions seem entirely frivolous. I came over here expecting to spend a lot of time reading and thinking. This is the last thing I expected." His important questions of the search came to an abrupt end in the face of some harsh realities of creating an adult life structure.

Often persons who have been known as searchers become, on entering young adulthood, more like unquestioning children than critical adolescents. "There are too many bills to pay to spend much time reflecting on faith." According to Vaillant the concerns of "making it" tend to lead to self-deception, dullness, conformity, colorlessness, and blandness. These words may indeed describe the nature of Christian faith as expressed by young adults. They tend to be conforming in their faith, following the latest fads and simple solutions. They like to believe that they are spending much time on faith issues when they are really spending much time "doing" church

9. Vaillant, *Adaptation to Life*, p. 202.

work. In the face of the pressures of love and work, they have little time for critical reflection.

They also tend to associate with Christians who are like themselves. This can lead to elitism. When someone enters their group who does not quite fit, for whatever reasons, there can be either subtle or overt pressure for them to leave.

It seems that the primary crisis in young adulthood is the kingdom of God versus the kingdom of the world. This is true in relation to intimacy issues. Today marriage is not taken seriously. Culture shouts that the individual is most important and that a marriage relationship is worth maintaining only if it furthers one's own well-being. The Christian teaching on marriage is much more like Erikson's notion of intimacy. We are created to be in relationship, and relationships will cost us something. We choose to be in relationship; therefore we are responsible for the well-being of that relationship. The same is true of friendships. These relationships are given to us to help us live out the gospel. Today, relationships seem to be important only if the other person is important. Friendships are not understood in the language of community but in the language of networking. The kingdom of God calls us to understand the mutual and reciprocal nature of relationships and to live in community with others and in covenant with spouses. The kingdom of this world beckons us to use others and to contract with our spouses.

At work the crisis is the same. The kingdom of the world calls us to seek jobs in which we will make the most money. It calls us to embark on careers that may cause us to hurt others as we advance. It calls us to be consumed with productivity but neglects quality. The kingdom of God, however, calls us to think of the values of the gospel as we select jobs, to defy the materialism of the world, to care for others in our work world and for the quality of our work because it can be an act of worship. It calls us back to the important notion of vocation, what Walter Brueggemann calls "a purpose for being in the world that is related to the purposes of God."[10]

What then is the task of Christian formation in this cycle of consolidating versus fragmenting? Primarily it is to keep in focus the gains of Christian maturing that, we hope, were won in the searching cycle. These gains seem to be those that help us to remember the kingdom of God as we are in intimate relationships and as we con-

10. Walter Brueggemann, "Covenanting as Human Vocation," *Interpretation* 33, 2 (April 1979): 115–29.

sider vocation. If someone takes a career simply for the material returns when she has come to understand the call of the gospel to care for others, then she has lost the gains of Christian formation. The task is also to find time in the busyness of creating the adult life structure to remember God. This does not mean simply going to church, although it includes that. It means keeping your Christian faith in the center of your life structure. It is fine that critical reflection sleeps for a while. We all need rest from the perplexing questions of life. But we must always remember our God. We must also be ready, for in the next cycle the questions will return. If consolidation does not occur, then fragmentation will. This implies young adults' inability to pull things together. They will be elitist and fearful of relationships. They will be unable to understand Christian faith as the centering component of life.

Reappraising versus Re-entrenchment

If we wanted to continue the river metaphor we might say something like, "Just when we think the river is safe, we drift around a bend and a new set of rapids is upon us!" It does appear that the general drift of adult life is from the calm task orientation in young adulthood to a new search for self and meaning in middle adulthood. Much mythology has been developed over the last ten to twenty years concerning the midlife years. One begins to think that it is mandatory to act like a selfish child in order to be a "successful" middle-aged adult. But like all good mythology, the literature carries much truth. The dramatic crises that have been popularized are much less frequent than the quiet crises most adults experience.

This period functions as something of a second adolescence. Vaillant writes, "As adolescence is a period for acknowledging parental flaws and discovering the truth about childhood, so the forties are a time for reassessing and reordering the truth about adolescence and young adulthood."[11] Middle-aged adults often awake to realize that the supposed need to work hard has led them to miss out on much of life. They often feel duped. They thought they were working so hard in order to create space in the future for play and family, but when they got there they were too tired to play and the family was gone or too busy. As the song puts it, "When you coming home

11. Vaillant, *Adaptation to Life*, p. 220.

dad? I don't know when, but we'll get together then." "Then" never arrives. This causes middle-aged adults to begin to reconsider who they are and what they will do with the rest of their lives. We call this cycle of Christian formation reappraisal versus re-entrenching. The nature of the task is to reappraise life to this point in order to renew one's direction and faith. The fear is that when one faces these issues, he will be unable or unwilling to creatively embrace the challenge and so will re-entrench in old ways of living and being as a Christian. We move now to a discussion of the issues of middle adulthood with implications for Christian formation.

Generativity

Erikson identifies the psychosocial crisis of this period as generativity versus self-absorption. By generativity he means a concern to guide the next generation. This includes the notions of procreativity, productivity, and creativity. At its root, generativity is generating offspring and nurturing them to a healthy life. If people do not have children of their own, then this form of generativity may find its outlet in the care of others' children. Productivity is producing things and ideas that contribute to the well-being of one's community. Studies of professional productivity indicate that most people are at their peak in producing good products and ideas during middle adulthood. We can hope that these products and children are developed with a sense of creativity. Creativity is the act of creating as well as style in creation.

If one resolves this crisis negatively, then one is characterized by self-absorption. Erikson has also referred to this as stagnation and impoverishment: "Individuals, then, often begin to indulge themselves as if they were their own—or one another's—one and only child. . . ."[12] Christopher Lasch has characterized our culture as narcissistic. Robert N. Bellah likewise has identified our culture as most concerned about individualism. Indeed, according to Erikson, our culture's major problem is its self-absorption. Each of these points to people who are more concerned about themselves than about others. They are treating themselves as their one and only child. We do so to the peril of future generations. Persons who become self-absorbed cannot nurture and care for their offspring or their products. They simply use both, if possible, to their own advantage.

If a positive resolution is achieved, then the resulting virtue is

12. Erikson, *Childhood and Society*, p. 267.

care. "Care is the widening concern for what has been generated by love, necessity, or accident; it overcomes the ambivalence adhering to irreversible obligation."[13] We may produce children or products, but do we care for them? Often care can only be given at a cost to oneself. True care willingly bears the cost. If we do not care, then we develop the vice of rejectivity. Rejectivity is the rejection of what we or others have generated, an unwillingness to care for the future generation.

The ritualization of this crisis is the generative act. By this Erikson means that middle-aged adults are keepers of ritual and tradition. They are the ritualizers. They generate traditions to carry on what is of worth in life. They coordinate rituals for the young so that their lives have meaningful ritualizations. But they can do this only if they care about the upcoming generation. If not, the resulting ritualism is authoritism. This is the "ungenerous and ungenerative use of sheer power for the regimentation of economic and familial life."[14] These are adults who control others and things by force in order to have their needs met.

Robert Peck expands on the issues at stake in this crisis. He claims that the middle-aged adult faces four challenges.[15] First, he must deal with the need to value wisdom instead of physical power. It is a sad sight when an aging athlete is unable to come to grips with declining strength. But more than this, we all use our physicalness as a way of dealing with the issues we face. It may not be in the form of athletic skill, but it may be dexterity, stamina, and the energy to work long hours. If we do not learn to value wisdom in place of physicalness, then we will face real difficulties. Second, he must learn to socialize relationships in place of sexualizing relationships. Much adult development literature reflects a shift in the way persons interact in male-female relationships. This has implications for married life as couples come to know one another in potentially new ways. It also has to do with friendships between the sexes as, it is to be hoped, the sexualizing element subsides. If it does not, then there will be continued difficulty in developing these friendships. Third, he must develop "cathectic" flexibility or face "cathectic" impoverishment. By this Peck means emotional support. Due to the death of parents and the

13. Erikson, *Insight and Responsibility*, p. 131.

14. Erikson, *Life Cycle Completed*, p. 70.

15. Robert Peck, "Psychological Developments in the Second Half of Life," in *Middle Age and Aging: A Reader in Social Psychology*, ed. Bernice L. Neugarten (Chicago: University of Chicago Press, 1968).

drifting apart of friends, the middle-aged adult may face the need to be open to new persons who serve as close emotional friends. If he is unable to make these shifts, then he will face the situation of not having close, sharing relationships, which we all need. Finally, Peck speaks of mental flexibility versus mental rigidity. Often middle-aged adults are stereotyped as rigid and dogmatic. They are seen as set in their ways and unopen to new ideas. This can be true for a number of reasons, some legitimate, others not so legitimate. The difficulty here is the person who is unable even to consider new ideas. Each of these four challenges affects Christian formation, but this one may have the greatest impact. As new ideas of Christian faith are introduced, are middle-aged adults open to them, or are they simply closed to any new way of thinking or doing in the Christian faith?

Reassessment

In addition to Erikson's concerns about generativity, another major theme arises in midlife: reappraising and reflecting on one's life to that point. Bernice Neugarten speaks of interiority to explain what occurs.[16] She finds that middle-aged adults turn inward and reflect on where their lives have been and seem to be going. She also finds that a shift in time perspective takes place where adults begin to think in terms of time left instead of time since birth. Those whom Neugarten studied also report that middle age is the "prime of life." They are in charge of the community and have more power than they have ever had and probably ever will have. Vaillant's research concurs here in that his subjects, without insurmountable obstacles to overcome, reported that they were the happiest at midlife. We must keep these thoughts in mind as we think about the reflectivity of middle adulthood. Often people think that interiority implies depression. This is not true, although it may bring periods of depression. People live their own life cycles and will face the issues of each cycle in their own way.

Also of interest in Neugarten's research is the report that women tend to view middle age as a period of increased freedom, while men view it as a time of increased pressure. For women, the children are or soon will be independent, and even career women find new freedom with the children gone. This tends to bring about a new identity search for them and can lead to their being much more assertive

16. See Neugarten, *Middle Age and Aging.*

and outgoing. In contrast, men begin to feel the pressure a bit more. They are concerned with continuing to be productive while at the same time beginning to look toward retirement. This often brings the feeling of two ships passing in the night. The male retreats from active pursuit of career while the woman advances. Many report that women tend to become more assertive while men tend to become more nurturing. This accentuates the diversity of direction and may help explain the high divorce rate during this period.

Levinson's work has furthered the notion of reappraisal as a primary descriptor of middle adulthood.[17] He divides middle adulthood into two phases: becoming one's own man and midlife crisis. Clearly we must be careful to consider the male bias that is in Levinson's research. He studied only men and seems to follow a psychology that holds up achievement and separation as the capstones of adulthood.[18] For theological reasons we cannot accept these as the goals of adulthood, if our theology holds relationships of care as central. Nevertheless, Levinson's work is descriptive, and many women find his description of self-reflection particularly useful. He claims that from thirty-six to about forty adults are in a settling-down period. The work of creating an initial adult life structure has been done; now one must live it. This is often a time of relative stability as persons work out their agendas. But around forty to forty-five, persons face the midlife crisis. This brings the reflectivity and reappraisal that characterize middle adulthood. The task here is to make some judgment on the relative success or failure of life thus far. Has the dream been met, or has it failed to come true, and if so, how do I cope with that? There is what Levinson calls a de-illusionment process. Once again, as in adolescence, persons must come to grips with those things in their own lives and in life in general that they wish were true but are not. They are not immortal. They cannot do whatever they wish. This reappraisal can be done calmly and quietly or can create considerable disruption for individuals and their families and friends.

In summary, we can say that middle adulthood brings two primary tasks: generativity and reappraisal. These can lead someone to become caring and thoughtful or self-absorbed and depressed. Cognitively, it appears that the possibility of dialectical thinking is strong in middle adulthood. Middle-aged adults have an increased poten-

17. Levinson, *Seasons of a Man's Life*.
18. See Carol Gilligan, *In a Different Voice: Psychological Theory and Women's Development* (Cambridge: Harvard University Press, 1982).

tial, most likely due to life experience, to recognize that not every question has one answer or even any answer. This allows them to think more dialectically and divergently. It allows them to live with ambiguity and paradox. If, however, a shift does not occur, then they will continue to be dialogical and convergent in their thinking. They will be uneasy with ambiguity and openness. Both the psychosocial and cognitive developmental issues have much impact on Christian formation.

Christian Formation

This period of the life cycle is characterized as the period of reappraising versus re-entrenching. Individuals faced with the issues of middle adulthood must also reappraise their understanding of Christian faith. They may face these issues noisily or quietly. As in adolescence, they may be very vocal and their faith may face considerable disruption, or they may quietly reconsider the foundations of their faith. The issues that precipitate their psychosocial crises are the same that bring about their faith crises. They have a deeper sense of the complexities of life. Having come to believe they had nailed it all down in young adulthood, they see the realities of life shaking the nails loose. Failing marriages, children moving away from home and Christian faith, suffering, death, and facing up to the reality of evil bring about the need for reappraisal. Success also can bring on faith reflection. As the song says,"Is that all there is? If that's all there is, . . . then let's keep dancing." Success may cause people to realize that there is more to life than the fulfillment of their human desires. Success or failure, faith must face up to the de-illusionment of life.

Middle-aged adults striving to be hard-working, firm-believing Christians wake up to realize that they will never be the "disciples" they thought they could be. "The righteousness we had hoped to achieve as disciples grows and kicks within us," writes Neill Hamilton. "We stop generating long-range plans and strategies for God and the Kingdom."[19] Middle-aged adults sense that they can no longer maintain this type of faith. Or, they might re-entrench to a simplistic form of faith. Faith faces the challenge of being thoughtful or unthoughtful. We can choose to think about what we believe, or we can regress to a childish form of faith. Sharon Parks quotes Oliver

19. Neill Q. Hamilton, *Maturing in the Christian Life: A Pastor's Guide* (Philadelphia: Geneva, 1984), pp. 98–9.

Wendell Holmes, who is reported to have said, "I do not give a fig for the simplicity on this side of complexity. But I would give my life for the simplicity on the other side of complexity."[20] This is the challenge: to work toward the formation of a thoughtful simplicity or revert to an unthoughtful simplisticness. Paul Ricouer refers to this as "second naiveté," or the ability to reflect on complex issues yet find the peace that comes with simplicity.

There is also the challenge of faith being flexible or rigid. If we re-entrench, then faith becomes dogmatic and unmovable. If we reappraise, then faith becomes flexible. This is related to the issues of cognition in middle adulthood. Here is the possibility of dialectical thinking in the place of dialogical thinking. This implies the ability to appreciate paradox and uncertainty. Here we may also notice the effects of what Piaget calls "horizontal decalage." This means the extension of formal thinking into various content areas of experiences. Some people may be at the cutting edge of complex computer or scientific knowledge, yet remain very simplistic in their understanding of faith. It is to be hoped that middle-aged adults, in making faith flexible and thoughtful, apply all of their thinking abilities to the formation of a maturing Christian faith.

The issues of Christian formation express themselves in our personal lives, families, friendships, and vocations. We face the reappraisal of our entire sense of identity before God. For some this may lead to a conversion experience. Middle adulthood is a time when many report first coming to faith or experiencing a second conversion. For others it may be something like what Saint John of the Cross describes as the dark night of the soul. By this he meant the confrontation with the reality of ourselves, realizing that we do have a dark side and are capable of great evil. It is also a time of deeply facing who we are before God—alone, naked, and defenseless. In our family lives, we begin either to nurture a more thoughtful faith in our children or to become overbearing and turn to legalism. If married, we either enter a deeper relationship with our spouse as a person or seek to control and manipulate her. Our friendships can face the same situations.

When we encounter these transitions, we can either become withdrawn or enter conversation with friends about the transitions. If we choose to converse, we may face rejection by friends who have cho-

20. Sharon Parks, *The Critical Years* (New York: Harper & Row, 1986), pp. 50–51.

sen the easy path to re-entrenchment, or we may find soul friends who can speak to us about their own formation of a thoughtful Christian faith. Our sense of vocation will undergo change as well. The question of God's will may become more important, but not in any simplistic way that connects it to something like a cosmic game of Let's Make a Deal. We may find God calling us to or from particular occupations or ministries. Many middle-aged persons find themselves drawn to ministry; many move from lucrative professions to take up full-time vocational ministry. Others readjust commitments so that while they remain in their jobs they spend more time in their work for the kingdom.

Each of these issues is clearly related to Erikson's notion of generativity. Don Browning considers generativity the apex of maturity.[21] What are the direct implications of generativity for Christian formation?

First there is the issue of generating faith. Middle-aged adults are called to nurture faith in their offspring and others who are a part of the faith community. They are called to share their faith with unbelievers, thereby generating faith.

Second, generativity implies being co-creators and co-governors with God. We are called to participate in God's ongoing creative work and to assist in the governing of creation. This has implications for work in the church, in politics, and in the environment.

What seems bewildering about this is that we are called to generate faith in others right when we are reappraising our own faith. This partly reflects the paradoxical and processive nature of Christian faith. It is complex, yet it is also in process. We cannot wait until we have it all together, because the cycle of life and faith does not stop. This may help us to generate a more mature faith in our children as they watch us live with complexity and doubt yet affirm our deep love for God through Christ.

Christian formation must also be related to the virtue of care. We are called to care for our neighbors, our friends, our world, and our planet. This again brings up the necessity of personal and social responsibility as Christians. We are also called to care for the community of faith. This includes nurturing faith as well as using whatever gifts we have to care for the community of faith. It calls us to be people of hospitality. The good Samaritan may be our example

21. See Don S. Browning, *Generative Man: Psychoanalytic Perspectives* (Philadelphia: Westminster, 1973).

of the generative Christian. He showed hospitality to the stranger and cared for his needs. The caring, maturing Christian will do likewise.

Finally, there is the way in which we go about our faith lives, or our ritualizations or ritualisms. We will be either generational or authoritarian in our relationships. If we are maturing in our faith, we will exhibit love and grace in how we generate faith in our children and others. We will nurture people toward the kingdom. If we choose to re-entrench, we will be authoritistic: we will force our children to affirm the faith, or at least we think we will force them. We will, by violence, attempt to force people into the kingdom, which will leave us with people who are more prisoners of war than children of God.

The risks and rewards of the cycle of reappraising versus re-entrenching are many. It is not a simple, safe voyage we are on. Faith leads us on a journey with risks and the necessity of reappraisal for a maturing faith.

Anticipating versus Dreading

We live in an increasingly old America. The average age of Americans is going up. It used to be that when someone was sixty-five years old, he was near the end of life. Sixty-five is the traditional age for retirement, and in a society driven by work, when work ceases life itself is threatened. This may still be true for many, but it is not necessary now (and was not before, although it was understandable). Interestingly, when retirement has been pushed later, there seems to be more conversation about taking early retirement. Both of these are probably good. Later retirement acknowledges the gains that medicine has brought us, and early retirement reflects a growing realization that life is not work and there is much to be done during retirement.

The aging adult can either look with anticipation to this phase of life or dread it. Anticipation implies that a sense of personal identity drives the person, not some culturally imposed idea that one *is* only if one *does*. It is a way of being that proclaims that the person recognizes and looks forward to a new era of life and a new way of serving God. The opposite is dread. The individual dreads any change and cannot anticipate anything beyond what she currently is doing. It may be due to a preoccupation with youth or work, but it leads to dreading any change. This dread manifests itself in a person's spiritual life as well. She exudes dread in her understanding of God and how she lives her faith.

We now consider Erikson's contributions to understanding this period of the life cycle as well as some cognitive issues, then we integrate these to develop an understanding of Christian formation in later adulthood.

Integrity

Erikson describes the psychosocial crisis of this period as integrity versus despair. He defines integrity in a variety of ways in order to gain a sense of what it implies. He refers to it as emotional integration and a sense of coherence and wholeness. He describes it as "the acceptance of one's one and only life cycle as something that had to be and that, by necessity, permitted no substitutions."[22] This last description appears to imply determinism or fatalism, but it need not. It describes more the willingness to look back after the fact and recognize the successes and failures for what they are and to be at peace with oneself. The polar tension here is despair. Despair is the opposite of integrity: emotional disintegration, a lack of coherence and wholeness, and the inability to accept one's own life cycle. This yields fear and anxiety and is epitomized by a frantic fear of death. In despair one cannot be at peace with oneself.

The virtue or vice that results from this psychosocial crisis is, Erikson proposes, wisdom or disdain. Wisdom means, for Erikson, an "informed and detached concern with life itself in the face of death itself."[23] The wise man can laugh at himself and live in joy. Wise people do not take themselves too seriously. The corresponding vice is disdain. Disdainful persons cannot maintain a sense of humor and laugh at the realities of life. They are unable to deal with themselves less seriously; therefore they disdain themselves and others.

The ritualization of this period is philosophical. The accusation that someone is "waxing philosophical" implies that she is being reflective and thoughtful about life. There is almost a romantic sense to this as she sits back and contemplates life. What this brings is a lasting sense of hope and purpose. The danger is the ritualism of dogmatism. This is a compulsive need not to be philosophical but

22. Erikson, *Childhood and Society*, p. 268.
23. Erikson, *Life Cycle Completed*, p. 61.

to tell others what life is about and demand allegiance to these views. It is a rigidity by which individuals strangle themselves and those around them.

Cognitive Development

Cognition in later adulthood is complex. Briefly stated, there is no need for an older adult to stop developing intellectually, but there are new hurdles that make continued intellectual development difficult. Short-term memory becomes difficult, which makes learning difficult. There is also the possibility of physical deterioration, but this is not a foregone conclusion. Given the proper settings and experiences, intellectual development may continue, leading older people on to new insights. There is the possibility, if dialectical thinking is not a part of one's ways of making sense, that it may still be developed.

Christian Formation

We must begin to treat our older adults with more respect. This is true in culture and the church. They have much to offer in the church due to the potential maturing they exhibit. The questions here are, "What are the issues related to Christian formation? What is implied by anticipating versus dreading?"

Relating back to Erikson, the question of determinism and fatedness arises. Often people develop concepts of God as having determined the outcomes of their lives. There is a theology of control here that may sidestep issues that lead to the ability to anticipate further growth in faith. If God has determined the path to a point, then God will continue to do so. This may be a message of hope to some, but for many others it may be something to dread. Those whose lives have been less than successful, however that is measured, will fear the future. As they reflect on their lives, they fear, and as they reflect on life after death, their fear may turn to dread. What must be developed is a sense that God walks with us through life in partnership and is there with us in both the good and the bad times. We must develop the ability to wax philosophical and anticipate the reality of God's presence with us in the future.

The danger in waxing philosophical is that people may become more dogmatic and demand rigid allegiance to particular ways of being Christian. When people are unable to detach themselves and be reflective, they become rigid. When they take themselves too seri-ously, they impose unnecessary restraints on others.

Clearly, a maturing faith calls for wisdom. The notion of wisdom is rich with meaning and is central to a biblical vision of Christian maturing. In Proverbs, wisdom is to be pursued and found in the fear of the Lord. The wise person knows what life is about because she is centered in God. In the New Testament, wisdom is to be sought after and found in Christ. Both Colossians and James encour-age us to pray for wisdom so that we may live fulfilling and maturing lives.

It is in this last cycle of Christian formation that we come to the possibility of speaking of Christian maturity, not maturing. But it goes on; there is still process as older adults anticipate continued growth and service and eventually complete reconciliation with God.

So the cycles of Christian formation come to an end. This discus-sion of these cycles is an attempt to build an approach to Christian formation that grows out of a particular idea of what the gospel calls us to as Christians. It also arises out of an attempt to use an appro-priate psychology to describe the life cycle. There is directionality implicit and explicit to these cycles. They lead to a particular vision of maturing faith. They do not call for a pigeon-holing of individuals as some of the stage approaches may. They are primarily to be seen as a map of Christian formation that points the way for the pilgrim Christian. What remains is to address some general educational prin-ciples that flow from this understanding of Christian formation.

13

Education for Christian Formation

This book is an attempt to establish the boundaries of a practical theology of Christian formation. It began by addressing a theology of Christian formation that in turn was the basis for selecting a particular psychological paradigm that informs the approach to Christian formation. Then, an approach to Christian formation derived from the theological and psychological foundations was described, and cycles of Christian formation were discussed. What remains to be discussed is an approach to education for Christian formation.

A variety of labels could be used for this approach. Some would call it a developmental or interactional model of education, and that would be accurate. I prefer, however, to call it a pilgrimage model of education. This may be an overused metaphor, but it carries best the assumptions inherent in this approach to Christian formation.

To describe the pilgrimage model, we will discuss the following: aims or goals, student, teacher, process, curriculum, and the setting for learning. These categories are often used as key ingredients to educational approaches. In discussing aims or goals, we address the ultimate purposes of educating: what are we striving for in our educational efforts? In discussing the student, we seek to describe assumptions made about the nature of the person as a learner. What do we assume about people in the educational process? Correspondingly, the section about the teacher describes the role of the teacher in the educational process. What is expected of the teacher? Our look at the process examines assumptions about how learning best occurs given a particular understanding of persons and aims in education. How are the aims best achieved? Curriculum refers to the paths that are used to facilitate education. Paths include experiences, texts, and anything else used to lead one toward Christian maturing. The setting or environment denotes both the physical and the emotional surroundings of the learning situation. What settings are most conducive to education for Christian formation? These categories describe an approach to education for Christian formation. They will not be dealt with exhaustively, but I hope to say enough to illustrate a pilgrimage approach to education for Christian formation.

Aims

It is often said that the word *education* means "to lead out." Christian education then implies leading out toward Christian maturing. The fundamental aim of education for Christian formation is, therefore, to create experiences and environments that facilitate Christian formation. It is, as Craig Dykstra states, "helping people to live ever more fully into the maturity imaged in the faith's tradition."[1] Our goal is to assist people in their attempt to make sense out of their lives in the light of the gospel. It is a task that is greater than merely telling about Jesus; it is supporting people in their attempts to come to know Jesus. The task is to "awake in the people of God a thirst for holiness."[2]

In order to do this, education for Christian formation must be both priestly and prophetic. Priestly education encourages and cares for people as they attempt to mature in the Christian faith. It comes alongside someone who may be perplexed and in need of direction. It gently nudges people in directions that will enhance their Christian formation. Prophetic education, however, may need to shove people in the direction that will lead them into maturing. Maria Harris, in describing this element in youth ministry, speaks of the ministry of troublemaking.[3] Often our educational aims should make trouble for those with whom we are involved. At these times our

1. Craig Dykstra, "Faith Development and Religious Education," in *Faith Development and Fowler*, ed. Craig Dykstra and Sharon Parks (Birmingham, Ala.: Religious Education Press, 1986), p. 253.

2. James C. Fenhagen, *Invitation to Holiness* (San Francisco: Harper & Row, 1985).

3. Maria Harris, *A Portrait of Youth Ministry* (Mahwah, N.J.: Paulist, 1981).

teaching becomes meddling. Often we come to enjoy the particular place at which we have arrived in our pilgrimage or we become unable to move on. If a priestly approach is unable to move us, then the word of the prophet must come and call us to move on.

The leading out must lead not to captivity but to freedom. Often people experience education in the church as something that seeks to conform them to a sterile image of the good Christian. It leads them to a view of Christian faith that constrains them in ways that are often foreign to the gospel instead of liberating them. No one has done more for us in understanding the need for a liberating education than Paulo Friere.[4] He invites us to consider a form of education that helps people be free and take responsibility for their own freedom. In essence it is an education of empowerment. Education is power. We use it to hold others down and to build ourselves up. We use it to control others and to make ourselves feel as if we are in control. What education for Christian formation aims at is not the use of power over others but the empowerment of all. As we invite people to take responsibility for their own Christian formation, they become empowered. They become enabled to mature in faith and to assist others to do likewise.

The aims of Christian formation must also be age appropriate; that is, they must be understood in the light of a developmental viewpoint. Christian maturing means giving all we know of ourselves to all we know of God. There is a relativity that is conditioned on human development. A child who conceptualizes God as a big policeman in the sky is understandable, but an adult who continues to do so has a problem. This relativity of maturing brings about both relaxation and restlessness. We can relax when we know that we are accountable for where we are now, not where someone else is or where we hope to be later in our pilgrimage. But we must also be a bit restless as we are beckoned "farther up and farther in" on our journey, as C. S. Lewis puts it.

The Student

Students are pilgrims on their way toward Christian maturing. We must assume the best and trust that they truly desire Christian

4. See Paulo Friere, *Pedagogy of the Oppressed*, trans. Myra Bergman Ramos (New York: Seabury, 1970).

maturing. We assume that they have some understanding of the call of the gospel as it beckons them to form a Christ-like character.

Christian education should view students as persons developing through the cognitive and psychosocial stages shared in general ways by all human beings. Not only are our aims to be age specific, but our understanding of students also is to be informed by developmental considerations. This should yield a sympathetic understanding of persons and shape our expectations of children, adolescents, and adults.

Students are not, however, the mere products of genetic maturation. They are interactive with the process as well as socialized. Robert Havighurst speaks of developmental tasks being derived from three sources: physiology, environment, and personal aspirations.[5] By personal aspirations he means that part of the self that is best described as the ego. It is our identity that is more than the result of physical givenness and environment. It is what we may call the soul: what God breathed into humankind and is beyond our reductionistic attempts to control. Somewhere in the mix of all of this we develop as Christian persons. This interaction takes place in a particular time and place. The way we understand our faith is informed by the historical moment and the place in which we live.

We also affirm that students are created in the image of God and are fallen. Humans have within them the image of God, which leads us to a high view of the student. We hope the best, believe the best, and trust. Yet we also know that the image is corrupted, so failure will come. Students will deceive, because we all deceive. Students will ignore their responsibility to mature in faith, just as we do. We hold something of a realistically ideal view of students, attempting to hold in tension the image of God and the reality of the fall.

The image of God also implies that students are responsible selves. We may be lulled into sin by another, but each of us is responsible for his actions. H. Richard Niebuhr and Paulo Friere remind us of this.[6] Friere's notion of "conscientization" implies the call of critical awareness, which in turn implies our responsibility for our own lives and learning. Students are responsible for their own maturing in Christian faith. In the church we often forget this and go to incredible lengths to overcome their lack of responsibility, or

5. Robert J. Havighurst, *Developmental Tasks and Education* (New York: Longman, 1972).

6. See H. Richard Niebuhr, *The Responsible Self* (New York: Longman, 1963); Friere, *Pedagogy of the Oppressed*.

we simply do not believe that people are responsible for themselves. If the former is true, then we will only frustrate ourselves and retard the Christian growth of our students; if the latter, we had better reconsider our theology of persons.

If we view students as interactive and responsible, then we will also see them as meaning makers. Life is a hermeneutical question. From birth, infants attempt to make sense out of their experiences. People are attempting to understand the issues of life and to give meaning to it. We are not blank slates waiting for someone or something else to write meaning for us. We are actively engaged in making meaning. Jean Piaget titled one of his books *To Understand Is to Invent*. This title carries the important idea that if we are to know something we must individually deal with ideas and invent meaning. The writer of Ecclesiastes asserts that nothing is new under the sun, but for every human being the sun appears as brand new. The point is, we must each re-create knowledge in our own lives. We can be informed by the past and the experience of others, but we give the meaning to our lives. The power of the gospel is manifest as each person encounters the truth of salvation for the first time. Yes, it is an old, old story, but it becomes brand new as each person encounters it.

This encounter is also very personal, and the contents of faith must be known personally. Michael Polanyi addresses the problem of an epistemology that is overly objective.[7] By this he means that what people come to know is what they really care about. There is a deeply subjective side to knowledge that requires us to temper our fascination with knowing about things. Parker Palmer relates Polanyi's ideas to spirituality.[8] He finds it unacceptable to think of Christian faith in objective terms only, writing, "We undermine the gospel claim that truth is personal and communal (with all its attendant ambiguities) by embracing the rigid but reassuring notion that truth can be captured in propositions."[9] How inadequate it is to know *about* Jesus but not to *know* Jesus! How inadequate to know *about* Christian maturing but not to *know* maturing as a part of our life experience!

7. Michael Polanyi, *Personal Knowledge: Towards a Post-Critical Philosophy* (Chicago: University of Chicago Press, 1958).

8. Parker J. Palmer, *To Know as We Are Known: A Spirituality of Education* (New York: Harper & Row, 1983).

9. Parker Palmer, "Learning Is the Thing for You," *Weavings* 4 (September/October 1989): 13.

Students are pilgrims created in the image of God and marred by the fall, journeying through the life cycle, at a particular time and place, and responsible to make sense out of their own lives in the light of the gospel. This view of the student greatly affects how we educate toward Christian maturing.

The Teacher

I want to draw a fine line between the teacher and the process of teaching. Here we want to consider the person of the teacher, what she brings to the teaching process and what qualifications are necessary. Also important are the metaphors that guide the way we understand the teaching role.

If students are pilgrims, then teachers are co-pilgrims. That is, teachers, too, are in the process of becoming mature Christian persons. It is hoped that they are a bit more experienced in the journey of faith than their students, for as Laurent Daloz writes, "The appearance of someone who has already taken the journey can bring a sigh of relief to the best of us."[10] As co-pilgrims, however, teachers must understand themselves as still in process and appreciate each learning situation as a new part of the journey.

For the teacher to be a co-pilgrim is for her to acknowledge that she is a co-developer. This means that she is aware of her own development in the cognitive, psychosocial, and spiritual realms. Cognitively, she must be aware of her own meaning-making process. How does she think about issues? As Philip Jackson writes, "Teachers are no less caught up in the task of interpreting what goes on around them than are any of the rest of us."[11] This implies that teachers must be aware of how they are thinking and be open about this with their students. They are also dealing with psychosocial issues. They are most likely dealing with identity, intimacy, and generativity issues. This will affect how they interact with their students and can be either educative or miseducative. If they are self-aware, then they can use the teaching situation for the growth of both students and themselves, but if they are unaware, they probably will visit unwanted grief on themselves and their students. They are also in

10. Laurent Daloz, *Effective Teaching and Mentoring: Realizing the Transformational Power of Adult Learning Experiences* (San Francisco: Jossey-Bass, 1987), p. 27.
11. Philip W. Jackson, *The Practice of Teaching* (New York: Teachers College Press, 1986), p. 86.

the midst of their journey of Christian maturing. How they are living in the faith will greatly affect their ability to teach faith.

All of these issues call the teacher to be self-reflective. They call the teacher to an awareness that she is in the process with her students. She is a co-learner. She must recognize her limitations and display an openness to learning.

What qualifies one to lead another toward Christian maturing? Thomas Groome recently reminded us that the "heart of religious education is the heart of the religious educator." Clearly the first qualification to teach faith is to be in faith. If you are only teaching about faith, then the teacher need not be in faith. But if the goal of teaching is to facilitate the process of becoming more Christian, then the teacher must be on that journey as well.

Research on good teaching reveals two additional important qualifications: knowledge and enthusiasm. To teach Christian faith the teacher must know about the faith. This by no means contradicts what was just said. One cannot be in faith unless one knows what that means. The teacher, therefore, must know about Christian faith. This implies a knowledge of Scripture, Christian tradition, reasons for belief, and the experience of faith. Knowledge of Scripture includes knowledge of the contents of Scripture and of their proper interpretation. Teachers must be careful in their use of the Bible. They must also know the major movements of the Christian tradition. We often act as if the church were only a hundred years old. We must help teachers gain perspective by understanding church history. They must also be aware of the use of reason in Christian life. We cannot bifurcate faith and reason. Our faith must be thoughtful and reasonable. We must help teachers to be thoughtful in faith and not fearful of thinking. Finally, teachers must understand the experience of faith. They must have in mind their understanding of the goal of Christian maturing and the process leading to it. They must be aware of how they understand the events of their own lives in the light of the gospel so as to assist others in doing the same.

This leads to the necessity of self-knowledge. A teacher must be in the process of knowing himself better. This was already stated when we discussed the teacher as co-pilgrim, but it needs to be emphasized. Knowledge of self-in-process is essential to being a good teacher.

Finally, teachers must understand the teaching/learning process. This includes both theory and practice. What is their philosophy of education? How do they understand the process of education? What

techniques work best for this understanding? Knowledge of learning
styles, cognitive styles, human development, media, and all levels of
teaching techniques is important.

Enthusiasm is essential. Knowledge in and of itself is insufficient.
Enthusiasm in and of itself is also insufficient. But knowledge linked
with enthusiasm is indispensable. Enthusiasm is a passion for God,
for self, for students, and for teaching. It is devotion to the goal
of Christian maturing, and it is delightful. Teaching sometimes becomes less than delightful, but if there is no glimmer of delight and
passion then one ought not to teach. Enthusiastic teachers who care
about their own Christian formation will be good teachers.

What metaphors best describe the pilgrim teacher? First, the
teaching role changes with different developmental periods, but
overall the teacher is a model, guide, and advocate for the student.
No matter what the student's age, a teacher is to model Christian
faith. He is to guide the student in her attempt to become more
Christian and to advocate the student's endeavors. The role of the
teacher does, however, shift depending on where his students are in
their cycles of Christian formation. In the childhood cycles of nurturing, training/enculturating, and belonging, the teacher serves as a
nurturer, caretaker, and encourager. He is an instructor, storyteller,
and tradition bearer. In the searching cycle of adolescence, the
teacher serves as patient observer, careful listener, meaningful frus-
trater, and idol smasher. In the consolidating cycle of young adulthood, the teacher serves as encourager, instructor, mentor, and assis-
tant. In reappraising faith during middle adulthood, the teacher once
again becomes careful listener and idol smasher. Finally, in anticipating faith the teacher is a visionary, patient listener, encourager, and
comforter. Each of these needs full description, but it should be clear
that the various cycles of Christian formation call for different gifts
and abilities. Teachers must consider their own approaches and find
the cycles that will benefit most from their gifts.

Process

Dykstra understands teaching as the "intentional activity of one
person that consists of guiding the learning of another."[12] Henri
Nouwen states that teaching as a redemptive process will be evoca-

12. Craig Dykstra, *Vision and Character: A Christian Educator's Alternative to
Kohlberg* (Mahwah, N.J.: Paulist, 1981), p. 124.

tive, bilateral, and actualizing.[13] That it is evocative implies that it calls out from within another the potential for development. To be bilateral means to understand that both teacher and student bring something to the teaching act. Actualizing implies calling for new life now, not later. Teaching in the pilgrimage model implies a process that is intentional in its attempts to call out of one another the gifts and growth necessary for Christian maturing. This necessitates a particular epistemology, an understanding of the rhythms of education, and a general understanding of the process of education that follows these assumptions.

Epistemology here means the assumptions made about how we best come to know. The pilgrimage model assumes an epistemology that is personal, relational, and transformational. We mentioned in the student discussion that care must be taken not to treat knowledge as objective only. "Wherever a strict dichotomy between the objective and the subjective has obtained," writes Sharon Parks, "we have also exchanged wisdom for knowledge and moral commitment for method."[14] Particularly in teaching for Christian formation, care must be taken to realize that what we are learning is not only objective facts but also subjective knowing. We must treat information as a good friend, as Parker Palmer puts it. Whether we teach Bible or church history or theology, we must tell how the subject changed our lives. If we do not work with a personal epistemology, then we end up with what John Dewey called a spectator theory of knowing. The classic example is the armchair quarterback. He knows what play to call, where to throw, or where to run. His knowledge is impeccable because he is always right. He is right because of the multiple angles the cameras give him and the commentary given by the announcers, not to mention instant replays. He is also always correct because he is not actually on the field. The reality of several thousand pounds of human energy headed toward you can greatly affect your ability to think clearly! Unused ideas or untested assumptions are worthless. Alfred North Whitehead speaks of the problem of "inert ideas." These are ideas "that are merely received into the mind without being utilised, or tested, or thrown into fresh combinations."[15] Inert ideas of Christian faith lead to inert Christians. To

13. Henri J. M. Nouwen, *Creative Ministry* (New York: Doubleday, 1978), pp. 10–14.

14. Sharon Parks, *The Critical Years* (New York: Harper & Row, 1986), p. 136.

15. Alfred N. Whitehead, *The Aims of Education and Other Essays* (New York: The Free Press of Macmillan, 1959), p. 1.

know is inadequate. To know personally and to participate in the use of knowledge is to be about Christian formation.

Our epistemology must also be relational. The Hebrew verb *to know* implies a knowing that is intimate. It is used in reference to sexual union. To know someone is to know him intimately. Likewise, to know an idea or concept is to be in relationship with it. To be in relationship with a concept is to care for it, to be angry with it, to play with it, and to work with it. We must know our faith intimately.

Our epistemology must also be transformational. This means that to be merely informed by a concept is inadequate. We must be transformed as persons in our knowing. Granted, not all ideas lead to transformation. But the ultimate goal of knowing is, as Paul states in Romans 12:1, the transformation of our minds. James Loder has contributed much to our understanding of the process of transformational knowing.[16] He finds it a process of five movements. We begin with a conflict or a challenge of new ideas or experiences. We then take time to live with the problem, to discover the extent of the issues. Then we have a time of insight or intuition that brings the possibility of new insight. Next we experience an "Aha!" moment when we feel our new knowledge. Finally, we re-interpret our lives in the light of the new insight. We take time to be transformed through and through by this event. If this process occurs, then we sense that our knowing is indeed transforming. Our epistemology must be personal, relational, and transformational.

Our process of education must also be developmental in that it appreciates the rhythms of education. This implies that we take into consideration the cycles of Christian formation as well as the movements of learning within each cycle. Whitehead speaks of three such rhythms of education: romance, precision, and generalization.[17] By romance he means approaching concepts in ways that capitalize on the novelty of the idea. It is a time for falling in love with a concept. For example, early on we must help our children to fall in love with the Scriptures and not to be overcome by them. Precision is the time for exactness and careful analysis of ideas. Here is where we ask students to interpret the Bible and think reflectively and critically about it. Finally, generalization returns to the romanticism that we may have lost in precision, but with the added advantage of thoughtful and careful analysis of the issues. Here the Bible becomes alive and

16. James E. Loder, *The Transforming Moment: Understanding Convictional Experiences* (New York: Harper & Row, 1981).

17. Whitehead, *Aims of Education*, p. 15.

vibrant because we have worked precisely with it. Within each cycle of Christian formation it is necessary to consider the rhythms of education. There are opportunities either to introduce new ideas so as to have students fall in love with them, to dig into other ideas and work toward precision, or to generalize on other issues that can be precisely loved.

A process of education that is concerned about both personal knowledge and the rhythms of knowing will yield particular approaches to teaching. These approaches will seek both to support and to challenge the student. A supportive process will seek to build community and a sense of hospitality in the educative setting. Parker Palmer speaks of creating hospitality, by which he means creating a sense that all are welcome and are encouraged to be a part of the process. The process must support open inquiry. It must also encourage students to take responsibility for their own learning. It must convey the sense that the student is capable of maturing in her faith.

A challenging process recognizes that true learning occurs when the individual realizes that her current knowledge or ways of thinking are no longer adequate. Christians realize that in the face of suffering and death their notion of God is much too simple. It is in the midst of this situation, a teachable moment, that one can mature in faith. The process of education must challenge by presenting conflicting information and asking for critical reflection on the ways in which persons make sense of life and faith. This must obviously be done with sensitivity to the methods appropriate for different ages and with support for the student's effort to deal with the challenge, but it must be done. The most concise expression of this process is Thomas Groome's "Shared-Praxis" approach.[18] This approach is both supportive and challenging. It includes five movements of the teaching process: (1) Considering the student's present experience in the light of the content under consideration: How might a student be living with the realities of this issue? This is not a simple way to "hook" the student, for it truly prizes the student's experience. (2) Asking the student to reflect critically upon his experience. How do his experiences affect him? How does he understand them? (3) Considering the gospel call. This may include teaching a part of Scripture or theology or whatever, but it is the point in which the gospel version of the issue is presented. (4) Asking the student to reflect on his experience in the light of the gospel. Are there things

18. Thomas H. Groome, *Christian Religious Education: Sharing Our Story and Vision* (New York: Harper & Row, 1980).

he must change or re-affirm? (5) Asking the student to commit to
new ways of thinking and being in the light of the gospel. Groome's
model articulates a pilgrimage model of education that is developmentally sensitive and epistemologically sound.

Curriculum

Curriculum does not refer to the printed material for Christian
education. Printed material is only a tool of the curriculum. Many
Christian teachers have become captives to the printed material,
which takes away our right and responsibility to select our curriculum.

What is curriculum? It is a course to be run. It "exists in order to
provide guidance to persons on their faith journey."[19] It is a road
map in broad strokes that points individuals in the direction of Christian maturing. Curriculum must be derived from one's vision of
Christian maturing or the aims established for educational ministry.
In the model presented here, the vision for Christian maturing is
related to optimum human development. That is, it is both theologically and psychologically sound. It is also a vision that understands
faith as including the dimensions of right belief, right praxis, and
right passions. The task of curriculum formulation is to develop discrete components that relate to the vision of Christian formation and
are developmentally appropriate. This implies that curriculum must
consider the developmental abilities of children, adolescents, and
adults, then select the direction that leads them toward Christian
maturing.

Curriculum must also consider issues of learning theory. It must
consider a variety of ways to achieve its ends in order to be sensitive
to learning styles. One aspect of curriculum formulation is the selec-
tion of activities that are used to teach the curriculum. These must
be derived from a knowledge of learning theories so as to fit students, who learn in multiple ways.

Curriculum should be developed with Bloom's taxonomy of educational objectives in mind.[20] This taxonomy establishes a sequence
and sets forth the components of learning. It includes both cognitive

19. Mary E. Moore, *Education for Continuity and Change: A New Model for
Christian Religious Education* (Nashville: Abingdon, 1983), p. 175.
20. Benjamin S. Bloom, et al., *Taxonomy of Educational Objectives: Handbook 1:
Cognitive Domain* (New York: Longman, 1954); also, Bloom, *Taxonomy of Educational Objectives, Handbook 2: Affective Domain* (New York: David McKay, 1964).

and affective taxonomy. A curriculum that is sensitive to the taxonomy will take care not to ask persons for analysis or critical reflection on concepts they have not yet understood. Often curriculum is so concerned with critical reflection that it does not allow students simply to know the concept. Yet sometimes curriculum is satisfied with simply knowing information without critical reflection. The taxonomy helps us to be sensitive to these problems. The curriculum must also be consistent with the process of education selected. In the model presented here, the curriculum must not settle for mere information transmission but must lead to critical reflection and appropriation.

The content of the curriculum must be selected to educate persons in all areas of Christian faith. The model of the Wesleyan quadrilateral is useful. The content included should cover Scripture, church tradition, reason, and experience. Scripture clearly refers to the need for curriculum to teach the Bible. The church has used the Bible as the primary basis for forming faith. It must continue to see the primary aim of the Scriptures as forming faith. We must, however, use it in ways that are more developmentally sound and intellectually honest. Developmentally sound use of the Bible means teaching it in ways that lead to a mature understanding of the Bible and are sensitive to the developmental place of students. Often we teach the Bible in concrete ways to children and are overly concerned with theological accuracy; as a result, later in life the Bible becomes a stumbling block to thoughtful people. Developmentally sound teaching calls us to teach the Bible as story to children so that they appreciate the major themes of faith and are not burdened with theological trivia. This raises the issue of intellectual honesty. There is an unnecessary gap between biblical scholarship and the ways in which we teach the Bible in church. James Smart spoke to this problem over thirty years ago.[21] We fear that scholarship will lead away from faith or will lessen appreciation for Scripture. In so doing we continue the anti-intellectual fears of revivalism. We must appropriate the best of faithful biblical scholarship in order to overcome this problem. We must also ask that biblical scholars understand their work as being for the church. They must realize that their work is to approach the Scriptures honestly and to lead the church in understanding them as our guide to faith and practice.[22]

21. See James D. Smart, *The Teaching Ministry of the Church: An Examination of Basic Principles of Christian Education* (Philadelphia: Westminster, 1954).

The curriculum must also include an understanding of church tradition. This refers to both the history of the Christian faith and an
understanding of the rituals and practices of various traditions. As
stated before, it often appears that we think the church is only a few
hundred years old, and we proceed uninformed by our rich past. We
read only devotional literature written in the past twenty years and
neglect the wealth of older devotional classics. This results in a narrowly prescribed faith that is historically and culturally limited. It also
leads to an understanding of faith that is more interested in exclud-
ing others than in including all who name Christ.

We must also teach the particular rituals of our own Christian
communities. Denominations exist to emphasize particular aspects
of Christian faith. If we refuse to teach our distinctives, we have no
reason to exist.

The curriculum must also provide ways to assist people to think
clearly about their faith. Faith does seek understanding, and we need
to address ways in which people can reason through the difficult
issues of life and faith.

Finally, the curriculum must help people make sense out of their
experience of life and faith. People need to be aware of the trajectory of faith and what it means to be a maturing Christian. The curriculum needs to assist people in integrating life and faith. James
Fenhagen states, "This suggests an environment where the issues
that confront us, often leaving us paralyzed, are seen as formative
issues for Christian nurture and must therefore be addressed as issues
not on the edges of the church's life but at its very center."[23] We
cannot hide behind piety and avoid reality. We must be a center of
lively inquiry into the experiences of life.

Environment

Environment refers to both the specific settings in which education for Christian formation occurs and the environmental qualities
of those settings. There are both primary and secondary settings for
educational ministry. Primary settings include the home and settings
in which the primary aim is educational: Sunday school, Bible studies, and action groups. Secondary settings include all those settings

22. See Walter Wink, *The Bible in Human Transformation: Towards a New
Paradigm for Biblical Study* (Philadelphia: Fortress, 1973).
23. Fenhagen, *Invitation to Holiness*, p. 46.

where an indirect result of the activity leads to education. Worship is not primarily for education, but people gain education from worship.

What environmental qualities should exist in settings so as to achieve optimal educational benefit? The environment includes supernatural, physical, and emotional elements. The supernatural element is the Holy Spirit's activity in education for Christian formation. The Spirit cooperates with us in the educating act and thereby leads us in Christian maturing. What we seek is an environment that is permeated with the sense that the Holy Spirit is present and will guide us in our growth.

The physical environment must be comfortable and conducive to learning and dialogue. Cold, sterile surroundings dampen the potential for learning. Warm, active surroundings invite learning. If people are physically uncomfortable, they will be less likely to learn.

The emotional environment affects the feelings people have as they enter a place and attempt to learn in it. In order to facilitate Christian maturing, environments must facilitate relationships. Although solitude is important at times, Christian maturing does not occur in isolation. We mature in Christian faith in community and we must have environments that invite relationships to grow. This implies an emotional tone that helps people feel as if they can be vulnerable. If we do not know one another, then we will never be vulnerable, ask questions, and make comments. This points up the need for what Parker Palmer calls the creation of space.[24] There must be space for us to think and wonder and interact with the concepts being discussed. Our culture prizes busyness. It claims, "The more the better." The more information learned the better you are. We must work against this and create space in which people can think deeply and peacefully.

Finally, we must have an environment of expectation. We must expect the Holy Spirit to be present to guide us in Christian maturing. We must expect that those present desire Christian growth. We must expect that all who name Christ will see themselves as on the way toward a maturing Christian faith. The pilgrimage model of education for Christian formation is for Christians who understand themselves as being on the way.

24. Palmer, *To Know as We Are Known.*

Bibliography

Adelson, Joseph, ed. *Handbook of Adolescent Psychology*. New York: Wiley, 1980.

Allport, Gordon. *The Individual and His Religion*. New York: Macmillan, 1957.

Arlin, Patricia. "Cognitive Development in Adulthood: A Fifth Stage?" *Developmental Psychology* 2, 4 (1975): 602–6.

Batson, C. Daniel, and Larry Ventis. *The Religious Experience: A Social-Psychological Perspective*. New York: Oxford University Press, 1982.

Bloom, Benjamin S., et al. *Taxonomy of Educational Objectives: Handbook 1: Cognitive Domain*. New York: Longman, 1954.

____. *Taxonomy of Educational Objectives: Handbook 2: Affective Domain*. New York: David McKay, 1964.

Boyer, Ernest L. *College: The Undergraduate Experience in America*. New York: Harper & Row, 1987.

Boys, Mary. "Conversion as a Foundation of Religious Education." *Religious Education* 77 (March–April 1982): 211–25.

Browning, Don S. *Generative Man: Psychoanalytic Perspectives*. Philadelphia: Westminster, 1973.

Brueggemann, Walter. *Hope Within History*. Atlanta: John Knox, 1987.

Buckley, Francis J. and Donald B. Sharp. *Deepening Christian Life*. New York: Harper & Row, 1987.

Buechner, Frederick. *Wishful Thinking: A Theological ABC*. New York: Harper & Row, 1973.

Capps, Donald. *Deadly Sins and Saving Virtues*. Philadelphia: Fortress, 1987.

____. *Life Cycle Theory and Pastoral Care*. Philadelphia: Fortress, 1983.

____. *Pastoral Care: A Thematic Approach*. Philadelphia: Fortress, 1983.

Coles, Robert. *Erik Erikson*. New York: DaCapo, 1970.

____. "The Faith of Children." *Sojourners* 11 (May 1982): 12–16.

____. *The Moral Life of Children*. Boston: Houghton Mifflin, 1986.

____. "Psychology as Faith." In *Theology Today* 42, 1 (April 1985), 69–71.

Conn, Walter. *Christian Conversion: A Developmental Interpretation of Autonomy and Surrender*. Mahwah, N.J.: Paulist, 1986.

Daloz, Laurent. *Effective Teaching and Mentoring: Realizing the Transformational Power of Adult Learning Experiences.* San Francisco: Jossey-Bass, 1986.

Dewey, John. *Moral Principles in Education.* Carbondale, Ill.: Southern Illinois University Press, 1975.

Dykstra, Craig. *Vision and Character: A Christian Educator's Alternative to Kohlberg.* Mahwah, N.J.: Paulist, 1981.

Dykstra, Craig, and Sharon Parks, eds. *Faith Development and Fowler.* Birmingham, Ala.: Religious Education Press, 1986.

Ebeling, Gerhard. *Luther: An Introduction to His Thought.* Translated by R. A. Wilson. Philadelphia: Fortress, 1970.

Elkind, David. *All Grown Up and No Place to Go: Teenagers in Crisis.* New York: Addison-Wesley, 1984.

____. *The Child and Society.* New York: Oxford, 1979.

____. *The Hurried Child: Growing Up Too Fast Too Soon.* New York: Addison-Wesley, 1981.

____. *Miseducation: Preschoolers at Risk.* New York: Alfred A. Knopf, 1987.

Erikson, Erik H. *Childhood and Society.* New York: Norton, 1950.

____. *Identity and the Life Cycle: Selected Papers.* New York: Norton, 1980.

____. *Insight and Responsibility.* New York: Norton, 1964.

____. *The Life Cycle Completed: A Review.* New York: Norton, 1982.

Erikson, Erik H., ed. *Adulthood.* New York: Norton, 1978.

Evans, C. Stephen. *Preserving the Person: A Look at the Human Sciences.* Grand Rapids: Baker, 1977.

Fackre, Gabriel. "Narrative Theology: An Overview," *Interpretation* 37 (October 1983): 350–62.

____. *The Christian Story.* Grand Rapids: Eerdmans, 1978.

Fenhagen, James C. *Invitation to Holiness.* San Francisco: Harper & Row, 1985.

____. *Ministry and Solitude: The Ministry of Laity and Clergy in Church and Society.* New York: Seabury, 1981.

Fowler, James W. *Becoming Adult, Becoming Christian.* New York: Harper & Row, 1984.

____. *Faith Development and Pastoral Care.* Philadelphia: Fortress, 1987.

____. *Stages of Faith: The Psychology of Human Development and the Quest for Meaning.* New York: Harper & Row, 1981.

____. *To See the Kingdom: The Theological Vision of H. Richard Niebuhr.* Boston: University Press of America, 1974.

Fowler, James W., and Sam Keen. *Life Maps: Conversations on the Journey of Faith.* Edited by Jerome Berryman. Waco: Word, 1978.

Fowler, James W., and Antoine Vergote, eds. *Toward Moral and Religious Maturity.* Morristown, N.J.: Silver Burdett, 1980.

Freud, Sigmund. *The Future of an Illusion.* New York: Doubleday, 1961.

____. *Moses and Monotheism.* Edited by Katherine Jones. New York: Vintage, 1939.

_____. *New Introductory Lectures on Psychoanalysis.* Edited and translated by James Strachey. New York: Norton, 1933.

_____. *Totem and Taboo.* Translated by James Strachey. New York: Norton, 1950.

Friere, Paulo. *Pedagogy of the Oppressed.* Translated by Myra Bergman Ramos. New York: Seabury, 1970.

Fuller, Robert C. *Religion and the Life Cycle.* Philadelphia: Fortress, 1988.

Gillespie, V. Bailey. *The Experience of Faith.* Birmingham, Ala.: Religious Education Press, 1988.

_____. *Religious Conversion and Personal Identity.* Birmingham, Ala.: Religious Education Press, 1979.

Gilligan, Carol. *In a Different Voice: Psychological Theory and Women's Development.* Cambridge: Harvard University Press, 1982.

Gleason, John J., Jr. *Growing Up to God: Eight Steps in Religious Development.* Nashville: Abingdon, 1975.

Goble, Frank G. *The Third Force: The Psychology of Abraham Maslow.* New York: Grossman, 1970.

Goldman, Ronald. *Readiness for Religion.* New York: Seabury, 1965.

_____. *Religious Thinking from Childhood to Adolescence.* New York: Seabury, 1964.

Groome, Thomas H. *Christian Religious Education: Sharing Our Story and Vision.* New York: Harper & Row, 1980.

Hamilton, Neill Q. *Maturing in the Christian Life: A Pastor's Guide.* Philadelphia: Geneva, 1984.

Harris, Maria. *A Portrait of Youth Ministry.* Mahwah, N.J.: Paulist, 1981.

Hauerwas, Stanley. "Characterizing Perfection: Second Thoughts on Character and Sanctification."

Havighurst, Robert J. *Developmental Tasks and Education.* New York: Longman, 1972.

_____. *The Educational Mission of the Church.* Philadelphia: Westminster, 1965.

Helminiak, Daniel A. *Spiritual Development: An Interdisciplinary Study.* Chicago: Loyola University Press, 1987.

Howe, Leroy. "A Developmental Perspective on Conversion." *Perkins Journal* 33 (Fall 1979): 20–35.

Jackson, Philip W. *The Practice of Teaching.* New York: Teacher's College Press, 1986.

Jenkins, Daniel. *Christian Maturity and Christian Success.* Philadelphia: Fortress, 1982.

Kegan, Robert. *The Evolving Self: Problem and Process in Human Development.* Cambridge: Harvard University Press, 1982.

Kohlberg, Lawrence. *The Psychology of Moral Development,* vol. 2 of Essays on Moral Development. New York: Harper & Row, 1984.

Küng, Hans. *Freud and the Problem of God.* Translated by Edward Quinn. New Haven: Yale University Press, 1979.

Langford, Thomas. *Practical Divinity: Theology in the Wesleyan Tradition.* Nashville: Abingdon, 1983.

Levinson, Daniel J., et al. *The Seasons of a Man's Life.* New York: Ballantine, 1978.

Loder, James E. *The Transforming Moment: Understanding Convictional Experiences.* New York: Harper & Row, 1981.

Loevinger, Jane. *Ego Development: Conceptions and Theories.* San Francisco: Jossey-Bass, 1976.

MacIntyre, Alasdair. *After Virtue.* Notre Dame, Ind.: University of Notre Dame Press, 1981.

Maddi, Salvatore R., ed. *Personality Theories: A Comparative Analysis.* Homewood, Ill.: Dorsey, 1968.

Marino, Joseph, ed. *Biblical Themes in Religious Education.* Birmingham, Ala.: Religious Education Press, 1970.

Maslow, Abraham H. *Toward a Psychology of Being.* 2d ed. New York: Van Nostrand, 1968.

McClendon, James W., Jr. *Biography as Theology: How Life Stories Can Remake Today's Theology.* Nashville: Abingdon, 1974.

Merton, Thomas. *Life and Holiness.* New York: Doubleday, 1963.

Moore, Mary E. *Education for Continuity and Change: A New Model for Christian Religious Education.* Nashville: Abingdon, 1983.

Moran, Gabriel. *Religious Education Development.* New York and Minneapolis: Harper & Row/Winston, 1983.

Muuss, Rolf E. *Theories of Adolescence.* 3d ed. New York: Random House, 1982.

Neugarten, Bernice L., ed. *Middle Age and Aging: A Reader in Social Psychology.* Chicago: University of Chicago Press, 1968.

Neuhaus, Richard John. "Religion and Psychology." *National Review* 40, 3 (February 19, 1988): 12, 13.

Niebuhr, H. Richard. *The Responsible Self.* New York: Longman, 1963.

Nouwen, Henri J. M. *Creative Ministry.* New York: Doubleday, 1978.

____. *Reaching Out: The Three Movements of Spiritual Life.* New York: Doubleday, 1975.

Palmer, Parker J. *To Know as We Are Known: A Spirituality of Education.* New York: Harper & Row, 1983.

____. "Learning Is the Thing for You," *Weavings* 4 (September/October 1989): 6–19.

Parks, Sharon. *The Critical Years.* New York: Harper & Row, 1986.

Parks, Sharon, Walter Brueggemann, and Thomas Groome. *To Act Justly, Love Tenderly, Walk Humbly.* Mahwah, N.J.: Paulist, 1986.

Percy, Walker. *The Moviegoer.* New York: Ballantine, 1960.

Perry, William G. *Forms of Intellectual and Ethical Development in the College Years.* New York: Holt, Rinehart and Winston, 1970.

Piaget, Jean. *Six Psychological Studies,* ed. David Elkind. New York: Random House, 1968.

Polanyi, Michael. *Personal Knowledge: Towards a Post-Critical Philosophy.* Chicago: University of Chicago Press, 1958.

Poling, James N., and Donald E. Miller. *Foundations for a Practical Theology of Ministry.* Nashville: Abingdon, 1985.

Powers, Bruce P. *Growing Faith.* Nashville: Broadman, 1982.

Rest, James R. *Development in Judging Moral Issues.* Minneapolis: University of Minnesota Press, 1979.

Rizzuto, Ana-Maria. *The Birth of the Living God: A Psychoanalytic Study.* Chicago: University of Chicago Press, 1979.

Rogers, Carl R. *Freedom to Learn: A View of What Education Might Become.* Columbus, Ohio: Bobbs-Merrill, 1969.

Runyon, Theodore. "Conversion—Yesterday, Today, and Tomorrow." A paper presented at Minister's Week at Emory University, January 17, 1984.

Salkind, Neil. *Theories of Human Development.* New York: Van Nostrand, 1981.

Sanders, J. Oswald. *In Pursuit of Maturity.* Grand Rapids: Zondervan, 1986.

Selman, Robert L. *The Growth of Interpersonal Understanding: Developmental and Clinical Analysis.* New York: Academic, 1980.

Sherrill, Lewis J. *The Struggle of the Soul.* New York: Macmillan, 1954.

Smart, James D. *The Teaching Ministry of the Church: An Examination of Basic Principles of Christian Education.* Philadelphia: Westminster, 1954.

Steinberg, Lawrence D., ed. *The Life Cycle: Readings in Human Development.* New York: Columbia University Press, 1982.

Stokes, Kenneth, ed. *Faith Development in the Adult Life Cycle.* New York: Sadlier, 1982.

Stringfellow, William. *The Politics of Spirituality.* Philadelphia: Westminster, 1984.

Strommen, Merton P., ed. *Research on Religious Development: A Comprehensive Handbook.* New York: Hawthorn, 1971.

Sugden, Edward, ed. *The Works of John Wesley.* Grand Rapids: Francis Asbury, 1955.

Vaillant, George E. *Adaptation to Life.* Boston: Little, Brown, 1977.

Van Gennep, Arnold. *Rites of Passage.* Translated by Monika B. Vizedom and Gabrielle L. Caffee. Chicago: University of Chicago Press, 1960.

Wesley, John, and Clare G. Weakley, Jr. *The Nature of Spiritual Growth.* Minnesota: Bethany House, 1977, 1986.

Westerhoff, John H., III. *Will Our Children Have Faith?* New York: Seabury, 1976.

Whitehead, Alfred N. *The Aims of Education and Other Essays.* New York: The Free Press of Macmillan, 1959.

Whitehead, Evelyn E., and James D. Whitehead, *Christian Life Patterns: The Psychological Challenges and Religious Invitations of Adult Life.* New York: Doubleday, 1979.

Wilcox, Mary M. *Developmental Journey: A Guide to the Development of Logical and Moral Reasoning and Social Perspective.* Nashville: Abingdon, 1979.

Wink, Walter. *The Bible in Human Transformation: Towards a New Paradigm for Biblical Study.* Philadelphia: Fortress, 1973.

Wright, J. Eugene, Jr. *Erikson: Identity and Religion.* New York: Harper & Row, 1982.

Index

197